Dr. Gilat Trabelsi

Producer & International Distributor
eBookPro Publishing
www.ebook-pro.com

Adaptive Teaching
Dr. Gilat Trabelsi

Translation: Leilla Feldman

Contact: gilat.trabelsi@gmail.com
ISBN 9798796216637

This book is dedicated with eternal love to the memory of my late daughter Na'ama, who always allowed me, even at home, to be a bit of a teacher

ADAPTIVE TEACHING

A COMPREHENSIVE APPROACH TO
ACCOMMODATION TEACHING IN THE
INCLUSIVE CLASSROOM

DR. GILAT TRABELSI

CONTENTS

INTRODUCTION

"...There are those that have a monopoly on wisdom, and know better than I do, and know better than you do, what's good for me, what's good for you..." (In This Country, lyrics and melody by: Uzi Hitman 1989)

So, I guess not!

The knowledge, information, and tools out there in the field are available to everyone. They are nobody's personal property, and most of these things are not exactly something that could be patented, and that is a good thing. If what's mine is also yours, then the one who truly gains from this is the student. Every student.

The term "adaptive teaching" is not a new term in the history of instruction or education, but it has been updated and brought into focus in a variety of contexts that stem from social processes, cultural trends, and pedagogical innovations.

The need to provide a solution tailored to each student is a leading concept in the pedagogy of special education, but as educational and social awareness increase regarding the diversity among learners, the winds of innovation regarding pedagogical solutions blow for all. This approach is manifested in "Universal Design for Learning (UDL) (Ministry of Education, 2013), a model that is a type of architectural concept that assumes that the world was not designed specifically to fit each individual person. Any person might sometimes encounter problems with the world around them, and with the products they use. However, designers are trained, for the most part, to provide for the expected "average", even if there is no "average group," because every person is unique. The Universal Design for Learning Approach involves designing products or environments that suit a wide range of users, including children, the elderly, people with disabilities, people of unconventional sizes, sick or injured people. Universal design respects human diversity and promotes tolerance of all people in all of life's activities. It attempts to remove barriers to accessibility. As such, adaptive teaching is not "corrective", because no person is broken. Its purpose is to make learning accessible and appropriate for all students, subject to their goals, needs, and characteristics. It must be relevant for the student in an existing reality in an enabling environment, and it is an outlook from which ways and methods are derived. It is not driven by barriers of diversity or motivation, but by the thinking, behavior, and conduct of a teacher, one who teaches in an enabling educational climate, which is led "from above" and based on the principles laid down by the school.

As part of the concept of adaptive teaching, it is common to think of it as a "custom-made suit." However, a distinction must be made between personally adaptive teaching, which aims to provide expertise in a specific area, such as adaptive teaching of reading or arithmetic which is based on a professional evaluation; and tailor-made education for all, which is based on understanding UDL. Just as this is suitable for all teachers, it makes the learning significant and adaptable to most of the students.

Guidance on applications of universal adaptive teaching focuses on three main dimensions: the educator's thinking, behavior, and conduct.

The thinking of the teacher relates to the teacher's self-efficacy for creating significant learning and experiences of success for their students. This success generates their inner motivation to learn and develop, invent, adapt, ask and achieve. The teacher's curiosity arouses the students' curiosity.

The behavior of the teacher is based on the mutual trust between them and their students, on the unconditional love they hold for them, and on their honest intent to learn about their needs, characteristics, and areas of interest, and the issues relevant to their world, age, and cultural norms. The concept of an educator's behavior is based on the willingness to always keep learning, erasing presuppositions and, the obvious, trust in the natural developmental ambition of the student to succeed, receive positive feedback, and advance to a place that they perceive as being significant. This requires modesty along with leadership, knowledge along with being a life-long learner, attention along with listening, tolerance alongside setting clear boundaries, and a lot of faith in ongoing processes because this is mindful behavior, not magic.

Conduct, therefore, relates to the ability of the teacher to connect their thinking and behavior to practical applications of an educated multidimensional toolbox; a toolbox that allows them full usage with agility: to quickly retrieve, as necessary, the response to various functions and needs, out of cognitive flexibility, confidence from experience, and setting goals for adaptive learning and teaching.

On a personal note:

As part of my job, I stand facing school principals and their educational staff, facing student teachers in a variety of programs, facing veteran teachers, and sometimes facing policy setters and decision-makers.

Everyone wants to be tolerant, and many complain that they do not know where to begin or how to do it. They tend to ask, "Why aren't we taught teaching and learning strategies?" And "How is it possible to make all these adaptations in a large heterogeneous class?"

And I respond:

Heterogeneous? Does anyone know of a group of people that is not heterogeneous? Even identical twins can have completely different needs and interests.

Adaptive teaching also has adaptive evaluation, before, during, and after the process. The "before" is intended to assess the strengths and needs that will allow mapping the delicate human tapestry, set goals and methods; the "during" is designed to access the process, the way that sometimes also needs to change, as is the nature of a dynamic process; and the "after" is designed to assess the change, refine the elements that were found to be effective and helpful, and enable the setting of new goals.

There are no set-in-stone tips that are appropriate for any situation. There is a baseline where we meet the students. If we work to get to know them, we can adapt the manner, the method, and strategy for them and with them in order to lead them, in different ways, to achieve the same goal.

I am not judgmental nor the least bit cynical. From my many years of experience as a teacher, counselor, and lecturer, I know that whoever takes on an educational mission knows or will learn how to work creatively, while observing changing processes in changing groups.

The greatness of an educator is in their ability to ask for help, a behavior pattern that we would like to teach our students, in teamwork, and from experts in their field.

Goals of the book:

To reduce the anxiety of encounters that come with the demand for adaptive teaching.

To shape awareness and knowledge so that they move in the direction of a worldview connected to adaptive teaching.

To suggest examples for designing functions and skills, regardless of content or field of knowledge, based on accumulated experience, of many years, of experimentation, trial and error, searching, checking, evaluating, learning from others—including my students, and a lot of creativity.

Pleasant reading!

PART 1

~

ACCESS AND ACCESSIBILITY

CHAPTER 1

ADAPTIVE TEACHING FOR ALL – NOT MAGIC, BUT MINDFUL BEHAVIOR

The term "adaptive teaching" is not a new term in the history of education, but it is being renewed and clarified in a variety of contexts originating in social processes, cultural trends, and pedagogical innovations.

The need to provide solutions specifically tailored to individual students is a leading idea in the pedagogy of special education, and as social and educational awareness rises concerning the diversity among learners, the winds of innovation regarding pedagogical solutions blow for all. This approach is manifest in "Universal Design for Learning" (UDL) (Ministry of Education, 2013), a model that is a type of architectural concept that assumes that the world was not designed specifically to fit each individual person. Any person might sometimes encounter problems with the world around them, and with the products they use. Despite this, designers are trained, for the most part, to plan for the expected "average", even if there is no "average group", because every person is unique. The Universal Design for Learning approach involves designing products or environments that suit a wide range of users, including children, the elderly, people with disabilities, people of unconventional sizes, sick or injured people. Universal design respects human diversity and promotes tolerance of all people in all of life's activities, trying to remove barriers to accessibility.

As such, adaptive teaching is not "corrective", because no person is broken. Its purpose is to make learning accessible and appropriate for all students, subject to their goals, needs, and characteristics. It must be relevant for the student in an existing reality in an enabling environment, and it is an outlook from which ways and methods are derived. It is not driven by barriers of diversity or motivation, but by the thinking, behavior, and conduct of a teacher, one who teaches in an enabling educational climate which is led "from above" and based on the principles laid down by the school.

The thinking of the teacher is connected with the teacher's self-efficacy for creating significant learning and experiences of success for their students. This success generates inner motivation in both teachers and students to learn and develop, invent, adapt, ask and achieve. **The teacher's curiosity arouses the students' curiosity.**

The behavior of the teacher is based on the mutual trust between them and their students, on the unconditional love they hold for them, and on their honest, true intention to learn about their needs, characteristics, and areas of interest, and the issues relevant to their world, age, and cultural norms from which they came. The concept of an educator's behavior is based on a lifelong learning approach, erasure of presuppositions and, "the obvious", trust in the natural developmental ambition of the student to succeed, receive positive feedback, and advance to a place that they perceive as being significant. This requires modesty along with leadership, knowledge along with being a life-long learner, attention along with listening, tolerance alongside setting clear boundaries, and much faith in ongoing processes, because this is mindful behavior, not magic.

Personally, I believe that the first month of the school year is the time to establish trust and communication. A "courted" student will respond to attempts to know and appreciate them. If we give our students the feeling that they are valued, and that we are looking for their strengths already at the beginning of the year, and we are consistent in this, then during the year, even in times of crisis, we will be the meaningful adult they come to for solutions.

Conduct, therefore, relates to the ability of the teacher to connect their thinking and behavior to practical applications of an educated multidimensional toolbox. Conduct is connected with the ability of the teacher to join their thinking and behavior to practical translation of an intelligent and versatile toolbox that allows them to use with agility: quickly retrieve, as necessary, the response to various functions and needs, out of cognitive flexibility, confidence from experience, and setting goals for adaptive learning and teaching.

The various functions that adaptive teaching aims at are the result of the nature of the student and their needs. Everything the student does is attributed to learning, but the teaching compass seeks to direct the student to learn that which is positive and developmental. The delicate tapestry woven by each student's mapping of functions provides the teacher with the strength and faith to adjust to it.

Let us ask ourselves, what are the "materials that the tapestry is made of?" and let us map it: (partial gauge example)

	Cognition and metacognition	Attention	Friendship	Emotion and behavior
Areas of interest	☐ Educational ☐ General ☐ Personal	☐ Focused ☐ General	☐ Within the learning group ☐ Outside the learning group	☐ Empathy ☐ Listening ☐ Obedience ☐ Responsibility ☐ Stability ☐ Consistency
Strengths and styles	☐ Analytical thinking ☐ Synthetic thinking ☐ Creativity ☐ Verbalism ☐ Memory ranges and modalities ☐ Effectiveness ☐ Strategies ☐ Self-reflective	☐ Over time (how much?) ☐ In visual/auditory/movement stimuli ☐ Able to combine channels ☐ Regulates process and product?	☐ Leader/led ☐ Introverted/open ☐ Cooperative/individualistic	☐ Supportive/supported ☐ Helping others ☐ Knows how to ask for help ☐ Responsible ☐ Meets limits and rules ☐ Optimistic
Difficulties	From a neurodevelopmental source (congenital disorder) From an environmental source (differences, resources, support?)			
Are there disturbances? (Examples of questions that we'll ask ourselves regarding the student)	☐ IQ? ☐ Environmental barriers? ☐ Rigid thinking? ☐ Lack of proper opportunities for learning?	☐ Attention span ☐ Ability to focus ☐ Ability to shift attention ☐ Ability to manage and regulates attention	☐ Communication? ☐ Examines reality? ☐ Understanding of social situations? ☐ Norms?	☐ Objections? ☐ Barriers? ☐ Lack of knowledge? ☐ Emotional regulation? ☐ Post-trauma?

There are many questionnaires on the internet for getting to know students

Example of a questionnaire for acquaintance with your style, based on processing and accommodated work by Dr. Vered Shomron, with her permission:

GET TO KNOW YOUR LEARNING STYLE

Read each of the sentences and think about how it fits your style of learning. Mark beside each sentence the number that best describes how the sentence fits your style.

1=Never 2=Rarely 3=Sometimes 4=Frequently 5=Always

1	I can remember what the teacher said in class, even if I didn't take notes or copy from the board.
2	When I come up with a good idea, I have to write it down immediately or I'll forget it.
3	I get more work done when I work with others.
4	I remember words best when I hear them in a song.
5	I like to perform tasks step by step.
6	I remember information that I discussed with a friend better than information that I read.
7	When I try to remember a word, I picture it in my mind.
8	I prefer that the teacher teach the new words before I read a new text.
9	I prefer doing projects together with two or three classmates.

10	I have no patience to read or listen to instructions. I like to start working immediately.
11	It's easy for me to understand diagrams, maps, and graphs.
12	I don't like it when the teacher changes plans.
13	I need frequent breaks during the school day.
14	Figures and graphics help me complete tasks.
15	It's hard for me to understand people if I'm not looking at them.
16	I learn more when I study in a group.
17	I would rather have the teacher tell me the instructions than read them myself.
18	I learn by explaining the material to my classmates.
19	It's hard for me to sit in a classroom without getting up and walking around.
20	I learn more from reading about a subject than from listening to a lecture or discussion.
21	Sometimes I take notes and then never look at them again.
22	I can learn languages from watching movies or TV.
23	I enjoy class discussions and can learn a lot from them.
24	I learn best when the teacher explains the rules in class.
25	I learn better when I read over the material out loud.

IDENTIFYING LEARNING STYLE/SCORING THE ANSWERS

Now: insert your score into the table and add them up for each category.

Visual	Auditory	Sensory	Social	Analytical
7._____	1. _____	2. _____	3. _____	5. _____
11. _____	4. _____	10. _____	9. _____	8. _____
15. _____	6. _____	13. _____	16. _____	12. _____
20. _____	17. _____	19. _____	18. _____	14. _____
22. _____	25. _____	21. _____	23. _____	24. _____

If you scored 18 or more points in a certain category, it appears that you have a clear preference for that style. Consider adapting your learning to take advantage of that capability.

- If you scored 10 points or less in a certain category, it would appear that you do not like that way of learning, and it would be better for you to find a different way to learn.
- Sometimes, if the score is high in two or more learning styles, it is best to combine them. For example, creating graphics or figures and studying in a group.

After answering the questionnaire, it's a good idea to go over the class profile obtained with the students, as shown in the table below, and discuss the options for use in differential tasks in the class's daily routine or demands according to the data:

- Studying for tests together.
- Preparing joint projects and evaluating alternatives according to personal or shared preferences.
- Collaborative learning of a representative of any style in a "sub-group" and then teach in switched sub-groups (Jigsaw method)
- Practice expressions of "my style" and of other styles (like peer learning)
- Awareness of multi-perceptual instruction by a teacher

Visual	Auditory	Sensory	Social	Analytical
Ruti	Gadi	Tzvi	Nehorai	Ravit
Danny	Yuval	Yael	Dan	Hadas
Gila	Sarit	Yonit	Omer	Lior
Shoham	Chen	Boaz	Amit	Maor

However, teachers have various preferences, areas of interest, styles, and strengths, too. Thus, there is always the possibility "to tailor a suit for the teacher or the staff," both a solution for these aspects and combine it with a solution for methodical organization of the data (student profile, class profile). The earlier (stage in the year) we build a variable and dynamic acquaintance array with each student as a special tapestry, and with the group as a weaver of tapestries, the earlier we'll obtain a surer picture for the basic sense of confidence of the teacher, when we come to set goals for teaching. The more we collaborate and build a uniform language as teaching teams, our power will rise—initiatives, relevance, directions, interdisciplinary study, strategies, and solutions in problematic situations.

I would recommend that principals, before the year has started at the preparation stage, but also at any point in time: you don't have to wait, you don't have to have staff meetings to build tools to get to know your students. Familiarity with your students is based on their self-reports and focuses on their preferences for communication and learning modalities, and also on their hobbies, their favorite things, and more. All of these will serve us to create a methodical map and get to know the person facing us. When we have a map of the human tapestry, we have control over the conduct and a direction in which to aim.

So, what about achievements? Naturally, applying the right adapted elements raises the achievements of the individual, the achievements that are really suitable for measuring and teaching about the trend of cognitive change. **Of course, for adaptive teaching and learning, an adaptive evaluation should be used. One that indeed checks and evaluates the level of change of the individual in relation to the goals that were set, with the tools that were designed.**

CHAPTER 2

TEACHING TAILORED TO PERCEPTION AND LEARNING STYLES

A teacher is a better teacher, and their students are more successful in their learning, when that teacher is aware of adaptive teaching and intends to use it. When students believe that the teacher is "on their side", and is adapting the teaching to their needs and styles, they are more focused, responsible, motivated and committed to what they are learning, have a greater sense of self-efficacy, and are thus more independent (Tomlinson, 2008).

Adaptive teaching relies, among other things, on understanding learning and teaching styles that are based on knowledge from the field of brain research (neuro-cognitive science), on understanding perceptual and thinking functions, on terms that correspond to the learner's functions in the 21st century, and on the operations of expression and representation (Anderson 2016; Melesse, 2015).

Perception is not based on what we see and hear; it is based on our self-interpretation of stimuli we receive from around us. At school, these stimuli are usually visual or auditory. Thus, for example, a child who understands the Hebrew word "kibud" as refreshments, and is asked about respecting (kibud) parents, may well answer that "they are on a diet"[1], and anger the asker.

---

1   Translator's note: the word that means respect in Hebrew also means refreshments, and heavy/weight] (an old joke).

It is the same with the allegory of the group of blind people patting an elephant, who are supposed to decide together what object they are touching. Each blind person puts their hand on one individual part of the elephant's body, the tail, leg, ear, trunk, stomach, and tusk. Each one is exposed to different features, to a different experience of size, length, texture, and more.

They, of course, do not reach an understanding or agree that the object is an elephant, even though they know what an elephant is. The moral of the allegory is that when exploring reality, our perspective should be widened, and various outlooks and aspects be included. In this context, let us think of aspects that we use in teaching, and also think of advantages of cooperative learning.

Looking into sources of perception allows the possibility for anger at "the one we thought was the class clown." We'll expand on this in the chapter on the use of mediation.

Perception, as we said, is based on what is understood by the perceiver, and related to the learner's experience, expectations and context.... It interacts closely with the learning itself: while perception assists in developing learning, learning enhances the perceiving process. This is what we mean when we talk about transitions "from previous knowledge to new knowledge".

If we take into account that the world of the perceiver is constructed out of previous experiences and exposure to specific stimuli which are mediated by their senses; out of the context they create; out of the objectives that provide the reason they are in this situation; and out of their expectations, then we will remember that we have a variety of perceivers in the class and must apply multiple cognitive pathways to achieve the goal with the majority of them. We will talk about things, adapt our intonation, demonstrate visually through the use of the aids we have at our disposal, we will move and allow the students to move and be active in learning (more on this in the chapter about attention as a mental resource). The younger the kids are, the more we will be able to carefully and thoughtfully include experiences with taste and smell. The significance of perception, without the need for sensory input, increases with age. Thus, the student is capable of recalling, imagining, and relating to sensory experiences from different points of view and contexts. Perceptual learning allows using diverse combinations for interpretation and context.

In the introductory chapter (Adaptive Teaching in the Inclusive Classroom—Not Magic, But Mindful Behavior) we discussed the need to map the students' strengths, characteristics, needs, and difficulties. Responding to goals that have been formulated based on mapping is a combination of diverse elements in the art of teaching.

Below are two examples of style-specific response layouts and multiple perceptual-cognitive pathways which enable diversity in the ways of teaching and learning, enabling a variety of teaching and learning methods by applying accessibility and "coverage" of needs in a heterogeneous classroom. One is a suggestion for op-erative-strategic accommodations to the learning style, and the other is a mapping of means to process and recall the material, all based on the division into perceptual channels vs. mnemonic devices[2].

---

2   The word mnemonics originates from the Greek word Mnemosyne who was the goddess of memory in Greek mythology.

FIRST EXAMPLE:
ADAPTING STRATEGIES TO LEARNING STYLES:

Visual style

- Awareness of the teacher's body language
- Processing materials using graphic organizers: tables, flowcharts, mappings, diagrams
- Connecting learning material with pictures and illustrations
- Use of echo reading, following along with a finger
- Watching video clips related to the study material
- Learning using slide presentations
- Use of colors, for example, in geometry

Auditory Style:

- Lectures
- Class discussions
- Providing auditory hints
- Recording lectures
- Reading out loud
- Using jingles, rhyming
- Drama sketches

Senso-motoric activation Style:

- Employing the body while learning in the form of a game or any other regulated and agreed upon way
- Learning while walking and passing a ball

- Touching textured letters; wooden letters
- Use of arts and craft materials of different textures
- Use of doodles, illustration, sketching
- Role-playing, acting
- Performing guided experiments—the classroom as a laboratory

Social style:

- Study in small group—division into functions, cooperation, and more.
- Discussions and brainstorming while writing down ideas
- Cooperative learning—use of various methods, such as Jigsaw puzzles.
- Joint acting out of scenes from the study material.

Analytical style:

- Emphasis on organizing material before studying, planning
- During learning: organization in tables and charts
- Adhering to an orderly schedule
- Consistent work on every unit of material separately
- Covering study material level by level
- Meta-cognitive analysis and transcript of learning processes

SECOND EXAMPLE:
RECALL MEANS AND STRATEGIES: PERCEPTUAL VS. MNEMONIC DEVICES

Recall processes are closely related to the processing and organization of material. Therefore, material that was encoded, or that was arranged in a way that is logical to the learner, is more available for retrieval at the required time. The means should be adapted to the internal structure of the field of knowledge. It is preferable to start working with the student in the channel and style that work well for them, and later, we'll help them expand the repertoire of uses to additional channels and styles.

Means for visual recall:

1. **Acronym (a type of abbreviation):** Putting first letters of keywords into an acronym or sentence that is easy to remember. Examples:

   a. The necessary functions of living organisms: MRS GREN (Movement, Respiration, Sensitivity, Growth, Reproduction, Excretion, Nutrition.)

   b. Remembering the process for analyzing visual art (https://www.bespokeclassroom.com/blog/2017/1/10/acronyms-for-literary-analysis, July 17th, 2021) OPTIC (Overview, Parts of the picture, Title, Interrelationships, Conclusion.)

2. **"Stocktaking":** This refers to a conscious recall of a few elements, for example: in geography—recalling the number of seas=7. The retrieval is done by the cumulative amount.

3. **ID Card**: Recalling elements according to a repetitive pattern of characteristics, for example: five categories or set questions for depicting relevant content in history, with a preference for the quantity of elements based on short-term memory capacity 7 items +/- 2 items.

   Definition – What?
   Time – When?
   Location – Where?
   Background – Why?
   Participants – Who?

4. **Algorithm**: Construction of a navigation card, for example, that represents the fixed sequence of an operation, and facilitates following the sequence. This concept is taken from mathematics but is appropriate for many verbal subjects.

Examples:

- **Series of actions to solve an equation**
- **Series of actions to solve a word problem in mathematics**
- **Series of actions to analyze a sentence linguistically**
- **Series of actions in a biology experiment**
- **Series of actions in solving an "unseen"**
- **Series of actions in solving a multiple-choice question**

5. **Use of color**: Use of colors, just two or three, so as not to create over-stimulation, facilitates distinction for many students, and associates, for some, color with meaning. In teaching material using the classroom board, it is possible to convey emphases and distinctions via color, for example:

Classification Table in Science:

Animal (red)	Vegetable (green)	Mineral (black)
Red like blood	Green like a plant	Black like (volcanic) stone

6. **Use of organizational tools:** Putting coded words into an organizing pattern helps many times in organized recall and retrieval. The tool should be adapted to the nature of the operation, for example:

- Flowchart – For recall of chronological or continuous processes. Preference for a number of elements according to the capacity of short-term memory, 7 items +/- 2 items.
- Mapping of concepts, semantic map – for demonstrating relationships or links between concepts.
- Table – To compare data according to criteria.

7. Acrostic: Recalling content elements using vertical initials of the beginning of a row, for example: Memorizing parts of a subject by creating a paragraph/poem where the first letters of each sentence vertically create together a word that relates to the subject. For example:

a. How to write an acrostic creating the word acrostic (John Carter Brown, 2014) :

Acrostics can be
Constructed in a complex way, but
Really there's no need.

'**O**rdinary', or just
Simple ones, need only
The last, or the
Initial letter of each line to
Code for another 'hidden'
Sentence—like this one.

b. Using the word *think* to encourage thinking before speaking (https://www.google.com/amp/s/theacrostic-guy.com/2015/07/15/the-think-acrostic/amp/, July 17th, 2021):

Before you speak:
Is it **T**rue?
Is it **H**elpful?
Is it **I**nspiring?
Is it **N**ecessary?
Is it **K**ind?

Means for Auditory Recall

1. **Recall using a melody:** Putting words or content for recall into the tune of a well-known song that can be hummed or allowed to play "inside one's head", for example, recalling words in English or families of words according to a certain topic or category, each verse in a song is known for a group of words.

Recommendation: Watch the excellent example of "Ron Clark's story" (a movie based on a true story) teaching the names and sequence of the American presidents as a rap song.

2. **Rhyming**: Use of similarity between sounds of the end of the words to recall a group of related concepts, for example:

   a. **Processes of modernization in history and civilization: urbanization—accommodation—distribution**
   b. **Rules of strong emphasis in linguistic structures** – for example, a checklist for an essay writing phonetic device: "VOWELS":

   V- vocabulary
   O- Orthography
   W- Writing spelling corrections
   E- elaborate wording
   L- Lexical proper usage
   S- semantic clarity

3. **Self-hearing from reading aloud or speaking the material:** Preparing for a test that is based on the fact that the learner hears themselves saying the material out loud, or teaches a friend, or listens to a recording.

   An additional suggestion for a read-aloud card or podcast of deep orthography when teaching how words are read vs. how they are written, for example:

   gh- lough, cough, tough
   ight- night, fight, light
   Kn- Knee, knife, know

Means for Sensory-Motoric Recall

1. **Writing the material:** Many students remember the material only if it "passes through their hand", i.e. they must copy the material several times, or take notes in class.

2. **Remembering through parts of the body:** Use of points in the body for identification and recall, for example: Recognizing the difference between different letters by their shapes

   Or

   Use the first letter of a body part to associate with a conceptual list, even with an additional sticker over body part. For example:

   Literary concepts
   Arm- Allegory
   Face- Flashbacks
   Finger- Foreshadowing
   Skull- symbolism
   Mouth- Motif
   Eyes- Exposition

3. **Letters or numbers:** Honey or sandpaper: Use of sensory stimulation as channels for recalling priorities, for example:

   a. **Honey letters and numbers, like in the "room" method, to teach Bible for toddlers:** licking a letter or number written in their proper form in honey.

b. **Sandpaper letters and numbers, in a range of roughness-es graded from rough to delicate.** Passing a finger over the written numbers or letters.

Means for Recall through Logic or Giving Associative or Structural Meaning:

1. **Building linking sentences:** Putting concepts into the sequence of a sentence with meaning to remember them, for example: recalling the adjectives in syntax, in a pattern of 9 concepts=-2+7. "According to **time, situation, and place, I will decide (purpose)** on the **way of compromising on the amount** I want, **on the conditions** suitable for me, **and for the reasons** that are right for me.

2. **A trip in memory:** Remembering elements by positioning them as guided imagery on a fixed daily path, for example, the way from the house to the bus stop as a way to remember artistic means of poetry, in a quantity that matches the capacity of short-term memory. "In the doorway I left a **home/verse**, in the bicycle shelter I left **anaphora**, at the intersection with the yellow bench I left a **rhyme**, near the grocery store I left a **metaphor**, near the parking lot I left a **tone** and on the bus, I left a **skip**."

   Another way to remember by location is arranging your school day's Schedule:

   Home- history
   Bus station- Bible

School gate- Science
Class door- Chemistry
My desk- Math

1. **Building organizing means:** See the section on visual perception.

2. **Juxtaposition of concepts from the content with private associations of the student.**

3. **Connection to previous knowledge:** Connecting new material to familiar material for the purpose of recalling from existing knowledge, for example:

   a. It is possible to connect the situation in Germany with regard to antisemitism, Jewish history, to material learned on the situation of Germany after World War I (Unit E of the 20th Century, which was learned the previous year).
   b. Any interdisciplinary link.

Building "menus" for use in logic: Familiarization with a fixed menu of elements, from which it is possible to go out and change according to demand and teaching, for example: **building electric circuits** – if the student knows possible elements in the circuit, such as, power supply, three-phase, single-phase, resistor, coil, or other possible elements in a circuit, they can adapt them to the required circuit according to its name. Just like in a restaurant menu, you can ask for a salad with or without certain additions that appear in the menu.

The examples above are merely a small sample of a wide range which relies on the knowledge, skill, and creativity of the teacher, as there are no recipes, there is adaptation, and it's possible to combine them with changing objectives with suitable content and implement them within any curriculum.

MORE ABOUT CONCEPTUAL CONSIDERATIONS IN THE CLASSROOM

Organizing the board:

Board, yes, the board. How casually we use it or don't use it at all.

Assuming that now we are already more "multi-perceptual," and not only talking about it, let's think about it. Are we organizing ideas on the board? Are we summarizing information, and asking for it to be copied? Are we erasing? Is the board clean? Is the board organized? Is the board for us? Is the board meant for the students?

Advanced planning of the board enables us to focus attention on many elements in the lesson.

We start the class by announcing its goal, reminding the students of the current topics and the necessary equipment, writing the date on the top of a clean board and the lesson stages on the side. When we do all this, does the perceiver, our dear student, know what to expect? Will we be able to select the kid whose job it is to mark off every stage we complete in the lesson, maybe the kid who most needs to get up? Getting up with permission is not wandering around, and it is necessary for someone who needs movement and reactivity during the lesson. It could even gain positive reinforcement. It also helps us to stay coherent, connected, and consistent regarding the lesson we planned. Does that seem too practical? Try it and feel the difference.

For example:

Mathematics
Goals of the lesson: Calculate the perimeter and area of a triangle
Supplies: Pencil, ruler, eraser, highlighter, notebook

- Opening (review and background)
- Teaching the material
- Individual work
- Group game
- Wind down

We'll plan in advance, and consider also:

- Spacing, preventing visual and verbal overload (quantity), letter size, numbering, rows of text for copying.
- Logical use of colors—at least two colors to separate between "areas or parts" on the board, but without overload.
- Organizing means: tables, diagrams, brainstorming, conceptual map, geometric shape drawing. We'll use a ruler, if we want our students to also use it in the notebook, to encourage precision.
- Clear and proper handwriting (don't be embarrassed if you need to use a dictionary), use prepared cards or slides if your handwriting is not clear.
- Interactive use of the board and slide presentation or any digital application, assists us in remaining facing the students, remaining attentive to the class, to combine writing with a game, to invite students to the board for "getting up with permission" and more.

Worksheets:

Think for a minute: What are worksheets for? Do we always need them?

What's their objective? What will we do with them? Will we check them? Etc.

Besides saving a lot of trees and planet Earth, we should understand that worksheets are a means to achieve an end and not a goal in and of themselves. If we choose to use this tool, we must decide "what's accessible to whom." No one says all students need to receive the same page, because each student has unique needs with regard to: the way, the linguistic style, the quantity and pace, the visual accessibility, and any other attribute that is different between students.

Whenever all versions have the same goal, there is no reason you cannot design several types of worksheets, assuming that you first mapped the strengths of the students, or plan to specifically teach other styles.

A worksheet can be a very effective means for some of the students, and very frustrating for others. It has a title and a subject, as they all do, but a place for uniqueness: "Student's Name."

We'll use our judgment many times and in many ways:

What are the objectives of the worksheet: providing knowledge, an information sheet, text, exercising what was learned, review of the material, a quiz, a game.

When to give it out: Before we explain and instruct, individually, we must consider that if we gave out the sheet and we then want to explain it, some have already started to work on it. It is possible to project the worksheet onto the board and explain it before distributing it.

Is there variety and adaptation to age and capabilities: Varied tasks, activities, combination of cutting coloring, writing, gluing.

Is there accommodation of cognitive needs: language register, identity, knowledge, understanding, application, analysis and synthesis, evaluation and opinion, judgment and praise of new ideas, open questions, closed questions, with a list of words to choose from, without a list of words, with or without distractions.

Was thought given to components of the readings, layout, overload: size and type of font, density vs. spacing, with illustrations or without. We'll ask ourselves what the role of the illustration is, and whether it helps us achieve the goal or creates visual overload, boundaries between tasks, quantity of tasks on the page, maybe we should divide the pages into different parts, give out only a part of them each time, encourage challenge to differential advancement, maybe put together the parts we divided, bind them into a pad, and encourage discovery and a sense of moving ahead, and thus also have no need for the question, "What should someone who didn't finish do?"

Did we pay attention to instructions and questions: short, clear, separate and distinct. Preference for emphasizing activities or quantities required from the instruction.

Did we plan feedback, criticism, and internal and external control?: A worksheet that's left unchecked is like an activity that is incomplete or was never performed. It's like "a job that was done for no payment." We took the time to prepare it—let's take the time to check it. The student worked—they deserve for it to be checked and commented on. The type of feedback depends on the student's age, abilities, and how much we wish to increase the student's independence. We can comment in writing, we should also learn to deal with mistakes and corrections, and to provide feedback on that, too. We can check verbally with the entire class, we can invite students to check each other's work, or comment on answers in front of the entire class, and we can also enable self-criticism and self-regulation: before a page of answers, before a checking slide, before scratch panel, cumulative checking, putting a code letter beside every multiple-choice question, and composing a praise word from the sequence of codes marked, coloring the appropriate parts until receiving internal feedback, word, number, sign, and more, whatever you can imagine.

Did we find the right stage: a worksheet thrown into the rubbish, book-bag, or around the classroom, is like disrespect for my work or that of the student. What do we do with the worksheet when we finish – glue it in the notebook, file it in the folder, hang it on the class bulletin board?

References:

Anderson, I. (2016). Identifying different learning styles to enhance the learning experience.

Nursing Standard, 31(7), 53 doi:http://dx.doi. org/10.7748/ ns.2016.e10407

Melesse, T. (2015). Differentiated Instruction: Perceptions, Practices and Challenges of Primary School Teachers by Science, Technology and Arts. *Research Journal*, 4(3), 253-264

Tomlinson, C.A. (2008). The goals of differentiation. *Educational Leadership*, 6, 26-30

CHAPTER 3

MEDIATED LEARNING EXPERIENCE — THE LANGUAGE OF ADAPTIVE TEACHING

The Mediated Learning Experience is a cognitive theory developed by Professor Reuven Feuerstein. This theory, based on the works of Piaget and Vygotsky, posits that everyone has the ability during their developmental phase, to modify their behavior and learn flexibly through new encounters with the environment (Tzuriel 1998, 1998). The Mediated Learning Experience allows the individual to use environmental stimulation in changing learning situations; develop cognitive functions; build and process new thought schemes in a gradual manner; and create a system of needs for cognitive modification that is wider than its predecessors (Tzuriel, 1998).

The flexibility attributed to learning is a fundamental attribute of the brain. The brain can reorganize itself by creating new neurological connections, called synapses, throughout one's life. This flexibility enables neurons in the brain to create new connections and adjust their activity to suit new situations and environmental changes. Brain plasticity can be seen both by the creation of new neurological connections and the maintenance of the existing connection. Frequent use, training, and practice that rely on the student actively participating in a cognitive activity are both the "maintenance room of the brain" and the "department of development and assembly line".

The ability of the brain to change and adapt is a direct result of active learning, which includes both conscious and subconscious processes. The more we make the learning experience a conscious activity, the more we will be able to connect new knowledge to previous knowledge and use that knowledge in changing situations: we are able to adapt (Guterman, 2009).

The mediating language and its resulting actions are the translation of theory into practice. Its main advantage is that it does not depend on specific content and is usable in any situation.

Unlike the behaviorist agreement in which stimulus leads to reaction, our basic assumption is that between the stimulus and the reaction, many cognitive actions need to be mediated in the input, processing, and output stages. A mediator is a person who has the knowledge, experience, and tools to develop the thought processes of the student in all fields: academic, behavioral, emotional, social, attention, and so on.

Thus, for the environment to promote development, it is not enough to expose the child to stimuli and satisfy them; we must also have a human mediator in the form of an adult who is active and aware of their mediating role. Additionally, modern technology means that knowledge is constantly available, fast, changing, and dynamic. A high level of access to knowledge is available to the generation being educated today, and the relevant questions are: What do we do with this knowledge? How do we process it? How do we develop it? and how do we behave with it?—including from the moral and value-based aspects.

The mediation process is achieved by using appropriate timing, grouping and organizing the student's stimuli, blocking irrelevant stimuli, and putting them in the correct context.

The mediator has several roles:

- The mediator selects the stimuli, connects them to a frame of reference, organizes them in order, focuses the child on them, gives them meaning, and gives feedback to the environmental experience.
- The mediator directs the child's attention not just to stimuli they have explored, but also to the relationship between them, the order they are presented in, and the relationship between these stimuli, predictable results, and specific goals
- The mediator enriches the interaction between the child and the environment using elements that are unrelated to the immediate situation and that belong to the world of intent and meaning created from opinions, values, and efforts transferred from generation to generation as part of the culture (Tzuriel, 1998)

The acts of mediation, as defined by professor Feuerstein, are characterized by twelve categories. Many studies from the last decades point to the high availability of implementation and evaluation, especially of the first five categories:

- **Intention and reciprocity**: The intention of the mediator is to knowingly mediate between the child and their environment. The approach is adapted to the needs of the child and the ability they express, and it relies on the child's active reaction in order to achieve the reciprocity principle.
- **Mediation of meaning**: The intention of the mediator

is to give every stimulus positive meaning. The meaning connects to various feelings, such as feelings of importance, value, and continuity. The mediation of meaning is accompanied by situation-appropriate physical gestures, facial expressions, prosody, and intonation of verbal expressions.

- **Mediation of transcendence**: Instruction by the mediator to transfer and generalize beyond the current situation, time, and place. A form of thinking that implements consistent rules for circumstances and situations and creates an understanding that every experience exists within a wider context, and there is a causal connection between the events and processes they experience. The ability to create motivation for expectation and prediction is the basis for the creation of generalization processes and cognitive structures that expand with development.

- **Mediation of self-efficacy**: The mediator draws the child's attention to their ability to carry out an action and to achieve results, helped by encouragement and approval and, connected to a specific operation that indicates their success, using real, focused, meaningful reinforcement. Mediation of self-efficacy enables the child to believe in themselves and acquire a sense of control over their surroundings.

- **Mediation of self-regulation**: The child is directed to be aware of the need to adapt the pace of their behavior and the level of their intellectual activity to the level of accuracy required of them when completing an action or role, and to use reflectiveness and inhibitory control.

How is this done in practice?

Examples of expressions that promote a discourse of mediation: Intention and reciprocity (focus) -

- Maybe try starting with the smallest number?
- Are you sure the order you put them in is correct?
- What can you do to check your work?
- Like you did before... Do you remember?

Mediation of meaning (naming and excitement) -

- This line is called a horizontal line, and the other one is a diagonal line
- Wonderful! Look how clear it is when you use precise terms
- This is the amount, this is the color, and this is the length. You should use these terms.
- This is called a block and those are cylinders.

Mediation of Transcendence

- Where else can we use this rule?
- What do you think this is similar to?
- Which class can you use this in?
- How can we use this information when we need to calculate change?

Mediation of self-efficacy

- Well done! You did it all on your own
- You're making excellent progress!
- Wonderful, you're really making progress
- You defined that question perfectly

Mediation of self-regulation

- Be patient, try checking the data again first
- Wait, go over your work again
- Maybe you should try checking how many parts we need to assemble before we start?
- Let's take it step by step

Example for an assignment and discussion about transcendence: Find an equivalent from your daily life to every "rule" presented in the left column.

Compare with a friend's equivalents.

Rules that exist in school subjects:	This is just like... in daily life:
Example: In order to efficiently solve a division problem with large numbers, we will first reduce the numbers using the zeroes: $$\frac{1500}{300} = \frac{15}{3}$$	**Example:** In order to organize my room efficiently, I will first pick up the large items, then the small ones. This way, I'll be able to see the room and what's in it more clearly. As a result, organizing the room will be faster.
In order to fill a vessel of a limited size with both water and different sized stones, we first put in the stones, and then the water.	
To efficiently assemble a rectangular puzzle with many pieces, we will first find and assemble the edges.	
To help us remember, we will create an organized list.	
In order to solve a problem with four mathematical operations, we will use the basic rule: multiply or divide before you add or subtract.	

Suggestion for exercising mediation of meaning:

In the chapter about perception, we learned that "the experience of the perceiver" is what creates meaning. The perceiver's previous background, their conscious and subconscious experiences, their goals, their expectations, and their "goggles of reality" have important roles in their learning experience, their gaining of meaning, and how they can manipulate it.

The exercise: "A matter of perspective" is an old, familiar exercise that may serve the purpose. It improves the ability to communicate directly and clearly and to formulate precise questions. It can be used in many ways.

Every student takes a blank page. One of the students draws something. You can define a subject and then slowly encourage more free choice, according to the goal. The one drawing is the group leader. They must instruct the rest of the participants on what and how to draw what they have drawn.

In the first stages, it seems that the more the drawing is personal and complicated, the more different the original drawing will be from the results. That is all right. Here we can discuss everyone's uniqueness, the ability to see one reality in many different ways, and the legitimacy of highlighting the unique.

In later stages, we can emphasize the questions asked by the participants. The more precisely the questions are phrased, the more the result will look like the original. Additionally, we can create indicator lines for the group leader, which can be used as "road signs". For instance: paying attention to directions in the space of the page; defining the type of lines and their relation to one another, their thickness, and their amount; and the feeling the drawing created by connecting it to a familiar association. Every term we implement here will later serve to create focused thinking and to understand the role of the mediator, and how students can mediate for one another.

References:

Guterman, K. (2009), Hamoach Halomed Bakita [The Brain the Learns in Class], Hed Hachinuch, 84(1), 72-74

Tzuriel, D. (1998). Hishtanut Sichlit: Aivchun dinami shel yecholet halemidah [Cognitive modifiability: Dynamic assessment of learning potential]. Tel Aviv, Israel: Sifriat Poalim.

Tzuriel D. (ed.), (1999), Hitnasut Belemida Metavechet: Iyun, mechkar, veyisum bemishnato shel profesor Reuven Feuerstein [Mediated Learning Experience: Reading, research, and practical application of the theories of Professor Reuven Feuerstein], Kiryat Bialik: Ach

CHAPTER 4

ADAPTING MENTAL RESOURCES — GAINING THE STUDENTS' ATTENTION

My Ferrari

Attention is the mental resource of our consciousness: it is the mechanism, the attention networks[3], the fuel, the neurotransmission, the spark, the awakener, the brain waves, and the electrical impulse. When all of these work together in synchronism, we have a brand new Ferrari. A Ferrari that makes the right sound, has the right color, the right human engineering, and exemplary performance.

So, should we continue to develop it?

Reality teaches us that a significant portion of the educator's energy goes into constantly engaging and reengaging the attention of the learners: learners who are in a state of low reactivity levels and should maintain a constant level of attention. However, engaging attention can be taught, and the correct input will lead to positive results.

If we rouse the biological systems of input and arousal and focus the cognitive system of processing and mediation, we will obtain the suitable behaviors for the goals we have set: functional output.

---

3   Attention networks: sustained attention, selective attention, orienting, and executive control.

We will always focus our teaching on gentle tuning of the attention networks and mediation of the resulting executive functions.

The current theories in neurocognitive science characterize the human attention network as a system that contains several neural networks that address four different roles in the control of attention:

- **Sustained attention**: the ability to dedicate attention resources to tasks that do not necessarily interest the child over long periods of time while maintaining a relatively consistent level of performance. This ability develops throughout childhood.
- **Selective attention:** the ability to focus one's attention on a specified goal while ignoring distractions. In other words, directing the spotlight of attention.
- **Orienting:** The ability to focus one's visual and auditory attention while ignoring distracting stimuli and moving evenly between relevant stimuli: shifting and refocusing the attention spotlight when necessary.
- **Executive control**: the ability to handle conflict, organize and plan actions to achieve a specified goal, and the ability to regulate behavior.

Of the four attention networks, executive control is the last to finish developing (Shalev, Kolodny, Shalev & Mevorach, 2016).

We must not assume that the very existence of an attention network means that every student can control it to the same degree or utilize it for productivity. We must constantly teach and evaluate executive functions at any given time.

Executive functions are a collection of cognitive skills required to direct behavior, in any functional field, to a specific goal. The ability to direct behavior toward achieving a specific goal is the key to completing both educational and life objectives efficiently and successfully. Executive controls are required especially for functions that are not routine, well-practiced, and automatic; for new and complex tasks and processes that require awareness as well as precision and simultaneous execution. They include a group of high-level cognitive skills such as inhibition, working memory, cognitive flexibility which are aimed at planning, decision-making, self-control, and self-regulation.

Thinking, evaluating, inhibition, mental self-regulation, problem-solving, and others are characterized as 'cold functions'. 'Warm functions' are emotional self-regulation; management of emotions and delayed gratification; and congruence to situations we perceive as behavioral, emotional, and social (Ben Eliyahu, 2018; Margalit, 2014; Jacobe & Parkinson, 2015).

It is possible and even necessary to teach executive functions.

Do not let the apparent win. It is not at all apparent that students develop, spontaneously and without mediation, their executive functions in a flexible way to meet dynamic circumstances. It is not a given that they can transfer the skills between different subject matters and situations, and it should not be taken for granted that the students will "already understand from the example, internalize, and adapt accordingly".

We must teach students to practice, adapt, transfer, and put into practice the executive skills that stem from the high-level cognitive skills previously mentioned:

We will teach the students to **manage their time** using assessments, personal tracking, self-evaluation, and performance criticism. Additionally, we will teach them to **plan a sequence** of learning-related actions and work steps, such as the arithmetic order of operations, how to form and write a good answer, planning the steps to write a paper, planning how to study for a test, preparing a school backpack, preparing a bag and equipment for class trips, and so on.

We will teach them to **focus on the final goal** while minimizing distractions, raising and coordinating expectations, creating realistic and relevant goals, reflective evaluation of performance and output, making generalizations, and reaching conclusions regarding achieving later goals. These will also help the student predict how to behave in the future in similar situations.

We will teach students to **initialize tasks and navigate between situations and assignments by making decisions and prioritizing goals** while organizing the required equipment and the relevant space and thoughtfully choosing the appropriate skills and strategies. Sometimes, we will have to focus on the motivational reason for initializing tasks. This is especially true for students who claim they "don't always feel like it" or "are just not interested".

We will teach them to 'verbalize their internal dialogue': to think, explain, and criticize out loud their way of thinking, including their manner, emotion, intent, social situation, conflict, and so on.

This is not a one-time activity but work that is constant and difficult. It requires finding the best executive function for each task or activity. It is a process in development, and the rate of development might vary between students. The performance quality of the students will vary between them; however, tracking these skills can help both us and them in all functional subjects. Thus, we will be able to handle mistakes, learn from them and do better next time, teaching the student that "everyone makes mistakes, the important thing is not to make the same mistake twice".

We can create a tracking chart for every student. It can be digital, part of a reflection notebook, or a classroom board. In it, we will track and evaluate the progress of each student while taking into account their age. The tracking will be done by the educator alone, together with the student, or managed only by the student. We can also mark the progress down in the general evaluation when appropriate.

Example of a tracking chart (adaptable to your needs and requirements):

	Did this occur? (Yes/No)	In which context and Task?	Where else can we use this function?	Quality of performance (in your own words)	Quality of performance (numerical evaluation 1-5)
Time Management					
Task Planning					
Setting Goals					
Focusing on Goals					
Initializing Tasks					
Verbalization					
Self-Evaluation					

DOES THE BRAIN NEED TO REST?

As opposed to what many think, the human brain is constantly active. Without external stimuli, our brain goes into '**default mode network**', also known as '**wakeful rest**'. The rest is, in fact, a break from activities and external demands. During this time, the brain works intensively on the content that it has already absorbed. It processes existing knowledge; erases irrelevant data; activates associations, thoughts and ideas; consolidates memories; creates new and creative connections.

In our everyday life, the default mode network goes into action during breaks, moments of relaxation, planned times for thinking, and during sleep (Buchner, 2012). It allows certain brainwaves to rest: those that are needed for a cognitive-attention effort so that the system won't collapse when more brain voltage is required. Think of yourself as a student: if you studied for a test, didn't rest for a moment, and even memorized the material right up to the test, what is likely to happen during the test? Overload? A brain short out? A blackout? However, if you set a specific time to finish studying, let yourself have some time off for fun, rest, and relaxation, and arrive at the test feeling refreshed; miraculously, assuming you also took the time to study the content and context of the test, every word on the test lights up a memory and the answers pour out of you. Is it truly miraculous?

HOW CAN WE USE THE INFORMATION PRESENTED HERE FOR EDUCATIONAL PURPOSES?

At the beginning of class — "warming the engines":
The school day is built using transitions: transitions between

classes and rooms. Transitions require readjustment, sometimes even extreme ones, for example: from an active recess to a lecture-style class and, in general, from recess to class. If we use a constant ritual for starting class, such as a fun game or an activity that attracts the students' attention and subverts their motivation to keep playing or lessens the harshness of the transition, our chances rise for gaining productive teaching and learning time. We will create a habit of "warming our engines" at the beginning of our classes.

We can, of course, start the lesson using guided imagery, pantomime, listening to relaxing music, doing short riddles, spy riddles, or riddles with delayed endings where we only learn the answer at the end of the class.

Additionally, we can play a **preliminary game.** A game that invites students to participate in the interaction that is our objective, and brings it into focus. For instance:

The Numbers Game: Every child gets a number. They have to exchange that number for another while obeying two rules: one, you can't exchange it for neighboring numbers, and you can't give a number to someone who has already given you their number.

The basic version: "Five Changes to Nine", "Nine Changes to Twenty", and so on. If someone makes a mistake, their number is out of the game. Each time, we increase the speed and the number of exchanges.

The variations: We write on the board all the numbers of those who failed and are out of the game. In a later version, the students are required to remember rather than write it down, depending on how much mental effort we are aiming to use. We stand in a circle according to the order of numbers, or we stand jumbled up and switch places. The game can, of course, be played with the students in their seats, exchanging only the numbers between games.

A Serial Story with a Missing Rule: The teacher comes up with an opening sentence for a story. Every student continues with their own sentence while staying true to the context. The rule changes each time, for instance: you can't use words with the letter N at the beginning, middle, or end of the word (for preschoolers, the letter N becomes the sound N).

The variations: we can change the words and the sounds. We can add syllables or utterances, similar to Pig Latin or Ubbi Dubbi. We can speed the game up as we go.

Name that Tune is based on the tv game show. You play the beginning sounds from a song, and the students need to recognize the song by name. You can use songs from upcoming holidays, songs from the students' favorite genres, and so on.

Alternatively, you can use any familiar short game such as "Yes-No; Black-White, Who Am I?". Games that take no longer than five minutes and the entire class can participate as individuals or collectively.

Goal, process, equipment, and rules:

Classes are time limited. A sense of time is a developing ability and is not to be taken for granted. If we can focus early in the class on the subject, the main goal, the required equipment, and its sequence (See: example on the perception chapter), in the sense of "know where you come from and to where you are going", we will find that these road signs give our students a sense of confidence and expectation and an understanding of the beginning and end, and the ability to feel and estimate units of time. **This is relaxing. Knowledge is reassuring.** Early in the year, we might need a hall monitor to remind students of the rules and the time; however, at some point, it will no longer be necessary because students will develop an internal hall monitor.

During class — regular maintenance:

Spaced out teaching that includes breaks:
If we plan out different activity units, a class becomes more than merely teaching, practicing, or simply exercising. Class becomes like the reality we are educating toward: varied and changeable. If we divide the lesson into units of time and include interludes to utilize the default mode network, we will find that we manage to cover more material or, rather, have a more focused learning environment. For instance, we set a clock to ring every ten minutes. Then, we allow two minutes of previously agreed-upon activities. Music, dance, getting up, putting your head down, and any other action that allows the brain to rest until the next ten minutes start. We might experience fewer disciplinary violations, concentrated efforts, and a rise of abilities in all our students' functions.

Navigation cards:
We will create navigation cards and gauges for our students for new activities, processes, and skills they learn. A navigation card does not have a single format and can come in different forms. We

can create, with the students, a regular digest that will be on their school table during class. We can also make modifiable navigation boards for the classroom. When the steps of the process are present in the classroom, they become part of it.

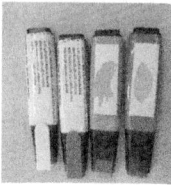

Example of a navigation card for reading instructions strategy and finding details in the text on the highlighters.
(Credit: Danny Cohen)

Image description: *Each Highlighter has the student's name on one side and the student's strategy in five steps on the other.*

Incorporating **gaming in teaching and using digital tools,** to the right degree, assists in increasing attention in class. These tools can help students practice and utilize strategies that will enable them to express their strengths. Additionally, we can use the same tools to evaluate their achievement of goals.

Providing **situations and roles that allow 'permissible movement':** games that incorporate movement, handing out pages, solving problems and demonstrating on the board, being in charge of the computer and the projector, and more all minimize free movement and allow us to direct the need to move about and recharge while receiving praise for their contribution and performance of duties. Even our controlled movement and use of sounds and intonation have a valuable role in increasing attention and alertness in students.

Delaying and pausing impulsive reactions are enabled both by the participation of all of the students in tasks that are hidden in communal applications, by using an eraser board, a marker, and presentations; by using and reusing pre-prepared signs of right and wrong, like a *dislike*; and by using age-appropriate pointers, a decorated popsicle stick that is on the table and used solely to raise one's hand. Every pre-agreed upon tool that is not part of the physical body forces the student to stop, think, plan, and make a decision.

Humor and writing jokes and riddles about the current subject promote **flexible thinking**. So do questions written by the students.

While performing tasks and tests, we should allow the students to use headphones or ear-plugs. If we can minimize auditory distraction or allow the student to listen to music that acts as white noise to screen out stimuli, we can see the student's performance change. **During the regular class**, a Madonna-like microphone for the teacher while students listen with wireless headphones will allow the student to pay attention for longer.

We can also allow the students to move in a personally timed controlled manner while using equipment specifically for movement:
Different uses for physiotherapy balls, balance training disks, standing desks, pedals under the table, and more (see examples for existing tools).

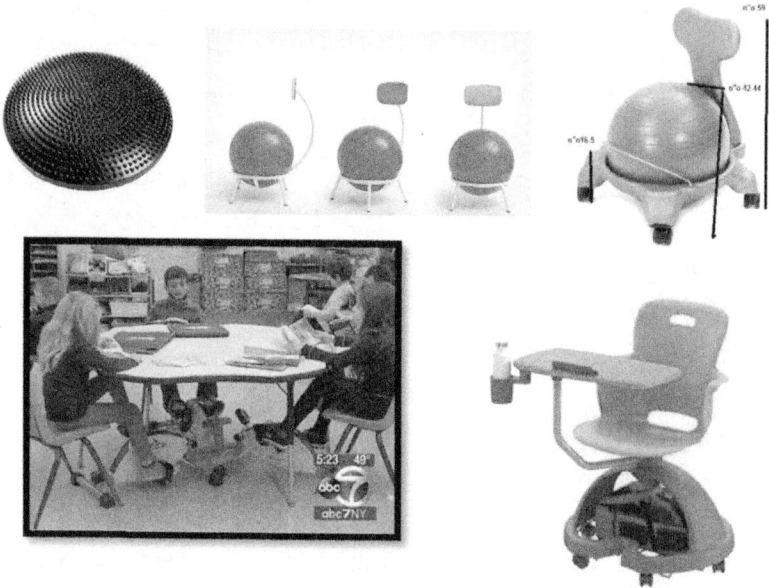

At the end of the class — summary and a preview for the next class

We must not let the end of the class simply end. The bell ringing doesn't "save the students" nor is it "only for the teacher". The bell is an agreed-upon signal that serves the default mode network and signals "stop listening" to the brain.

We must plan the summary since it acts as a link. It connects where we come from to where we are going. The class summary can, of course, change according to its content and goals, but several elements must be taken into consideration:

1. We should find out what the **students have learned from the class**, what they will take with them. This is something only

the students can tell us. We can do this by going around the classroom and asking the students, or in a game such as trivial pursuit or word association.

2. We should also find out what the students found easy or hard, did they gain tools from the class, and did they contribute. This **meta-cognitive reflection** is important as an evaluation tool for both the student and the teacher, less regarding the content of the class and more concerning the modality, the thinking processes that the student used, their inner exploration, both by themselves and with the teacher about different aspects of success strengths, empowerment, and focusing difficulties. We know it is important that the student be aware of how much they contributed to the class. The contribution can be active, such as participation, assisting the teacher or other students, presentations, and so on, or passive like summarizing the class, executing tasks, listening, and more, as long as the student is aware of how they conducted themselves and how much control they exert over the class. We can do this using the reflection notebook and by giving the students five minutes at the end of class to write in it or use another tool. If we have access to digital tools, we can work on a shared document in Google Drive that is accessible to both students and teachers. Once a week, the teacher can collect the notebooks and write back to the students about their learning process. At a young age or with children who cannot write, we can do this as an emoji chart with stickers or an audio recording to the evaluation.

3. We will manage **cognitive reflection**, especially after classes where new material, knowledge, and skills have been imparted.

After we taught and practiced the cognitive representation of the material, we will ask the student to write about the material from the lesson, in their notebook, the way it appears in their head using an organizational element of some sort like a chart, glossary, flowchart, diagram, and so on. With younger children, each child can have their own "garden of terms". The teacher can write with them on petals made out of Bristol board (or any other material) the terms they've learned or understood during the class.

Example of a reflection tool for young children:

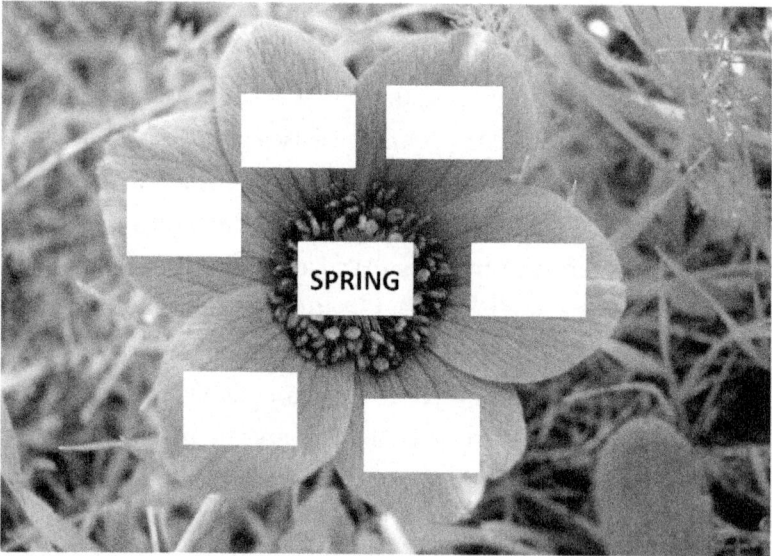

Example of a student's documentation
(Meta-cognitive reflective portfolio):

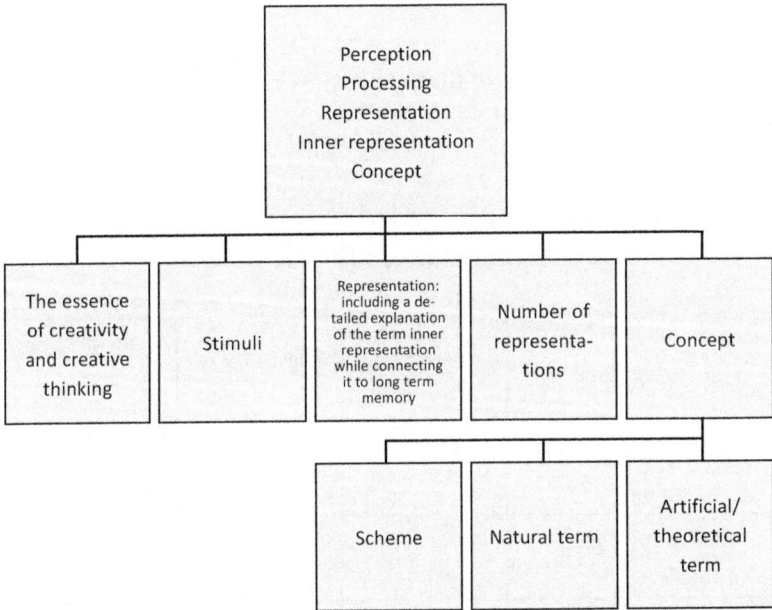

Perception Processing Representation Inner representation Concept

The essence of creativity and creative thinking	Stimuli	Representation: including a detailed explanation of the term inner representation while connecting it to long term memory	Number of representations	Concept

Scheme	Natural term	Artificial/ theoretical term

4. We will give tools for observation from outside: filming
   the lesson and analyzing it. Once every two weeks on an
   agreed-upon time, while explaining the goals to the students,
   we will film the class in a way we feel comfortable with and
   dedicate twenty minutes to choosing a random shot where
   a student observes themselves and summarizes their performance during the class in a chart. This activity adds an element
   of "myself in the mirror": a noncritical mirroring of measure-
   ments the student might not be aware of, with the ability to
   define goals based on personal insights. The criteria for the
   chart can be created ahead of time with each student or by

the educator alone, especially at a young age. There should be positive criteria in the chart. Additionally, the chart should also record the date, time, and subject so that both the student and teacher can compare different situations and discuss them.

Example of a self-observation chart that can be adapted according to the goal

Date: _____

Class subject:_____ **Time:**_____

The action	Mark ✓ when true	Summary of my actions:	Insights or goals for the future:
I raised my hand to ask to speak			
I focused my eyes on the teacher			
I copied off the board			
I participated in a group project			
I completed a personal task in one go			

5. We should find out how the student feels. Reflection of airing out emotions will be useful after a class that raises many emotions or causes reactivity to emotional situations. Taking into account the student's age or preferred style, we will ask them to respond to the class by precisely describing their mood or emotions. This can be done verbally, by using a round of emotions

stated out loud, by pantomime, by writing a note, by drawing, or in any other way. This type of reflection will allow the student to look inwards and release emotions and allow their classmates to learn empathetic behavior and communication skills, and allow the teacher to note red flags when applicable.

6. We will give a **preview for the next class**, allowing the students to know how this class will continue. As part of maintaining continuity, minimizing vagueness, and increasing the feeling of control over the process, we will inform the students what and how we'll learn in the next class. We must remember that planned continuity and knowing what is to come also reassures us, not only the students.

In conclusion, attention is a complex and dynamic cognitive mechanism. Every person has an attention profile that characterizes them, and it can be partially or completely controlled (with the exception of an untreated attention disorder of special educational needs due to a different neurodevelopmental disorder) by planning "attention promoters" in class. Of course, we will not use said promoters all the time and in every class, simply because this is impossible. However, if we vary between several promoters that suit both us and the students, use them consistently at different times, and learn to use them consciously, we will see that a habit and a discourse are created, and both we and the students have more control over what goes on.

The spice that will always enrich the attention situation is the amount of love a teacher has for their subject and teaching in general. The teacher's enthusiasm over their creation, i.e. the class, will make attention more readily available in the class.

References:

Ben Eliyahu, A. (2018), Niflaot hamoach haholisti [The Wonders of the Holistic Brain], Hotzaat Amazia: Even Yehuda

Margalit, M. (2014), Lakuyot lemida: model neurohitpatchuti - leachar 15 shanim [Learning Disabilities:a neurodevelopmental model - after 15 years]. Mifgash: Journal of Social-Educational Work, *22 (39)*, 15-34

CHAPTER 5

ENCOURAGING CREATIVITY VIA ADAPTIVE TEACHING

Think for a minute: How often does a lightbulb go off in your brain? Or you might have a sudden insight? Or something simply clicks? Do these thoughts come randomly, or do they have a trigger?

Creative thinking is not born in a chaotic, anarchistic, or spontaneous mind; chaos can provide the emotional or motivational base for reorganizing one's thinking. Creative thinking is a product of cognitive flexibility: creating new connections from existing knowledge, recently acquired knowledge, or from knowledge that is waiting for the right moment.

Already in the middle of the 20th century, researchers differentiated between two types of thinking:

Unidirectional thinking - a focused search for a single direction of thought in the existing knowledge reserves, convergent and focused thinking.

Multidirectional thinking - using various sources of thought and mapping them to unify the elements and create a new divergent thinking.

There are many definitions of creativity, most of which contain a cognitive element. For instance, one of the definitions in the

(Hebrew) Sapir dictionary is *"The ability to produce ideas and handle problems in a new and unusual manner."* However, problem-solving is not the only reason for encouraging and developing creativity.

Researchers from Oxford presented genetic findings from sets of identical twins about creativity, from which we can infer that creativity is a hereditary trait. However, researchers from other universities claim that while creativity may be inherited, its development into a useful skill depends on cognitive-educational causes.

The tendency of the brain to seek novelty as a thinking pattern that characterizes creativity has a dopaminergic source. Dopamine is a neurotransmitter in the human brain. Activating the brain in dopaminergic areas leads our thinking pattern to existing and new neural connections similar to a road or phone network. This divergence encourages out-of-the-box thinking. The combination of need, brain activation, planning, mapping, and connecting is the basis for innovative thinking. Most startups rely precisely on this type of thinking.

For instance, to invent the smartphone driving navigation app Waze, the needs rose for digital mapping, time management, improving commuting and driving decisions, and more. The activation process required connections between different sources of knowledge such as geography and mapping, algorithm calculation, software, UX, and so on. The precise planning and constant evaluation while changing and updating the program to suit real-world needs enabled the creation of a creative process and novel product that is constantly evolving. As a result, the program is a worldwide success.

The business world is also constantly evolving and therefore appreciates and rewards creative initiatives and solutions. A good example of this is a story about a man who made a large profit for himself and his company by thinking in an innovative way and coming up with a seemingly small idea. This man suggested to a well-known toothpaste brand to modify the opening of the toothpaste tube to be one millimeter larger. He also presented the company with the calculations for the resulting rise in the rate of toothpaste use. Thus, his idea raised the company's sales and profits.

Kaniel (2006, 2009) talks about teaching minimalist thinking as part of teaching knowledge and teaching maximal thinking as a thing unto itself. In the minimalist context, he claims that: *"The basis of thinking is the transference to different fields within each subject and within different subjects. The natural tendency is not to transfer and, to achieve it, one must put energy into transference."* About the maximal context, he says: *"Thinking is not a spice for the subjects, but another main dish. Therefore, one must specialize in complex thinking the way one would in any other discipline."*

Often, I meet teachers and students of education that declare, in the first meeting, "I am not creative." When I ask what they mean by this, they say, "I have two left hands": they feel they lack artistic talent, and sometimes have low motivation to innovate: no desire to reinvent the wheel or dare to try something new in class.

It is clear to me today that in order to encourage inner motivation and lower the anxiety of the educator, one needs to have a sense of ability alongside the experience of success. Together, these feelings feed each other and create a new experience of teaching and learning.

Bandura defines 'self-efficacy' as "an individual's belief in his or her capacity to execute behaviors necessary to produce specific performance attainments (Bandura, 1977, 1986, 1997). Self-efficacy reflects confidence in the ability to exert control over one's own motivation, behavior, and social environment." In other words, people will complete a task only if they believe it matches the ability they think they have, and will avoid a task they feel is too big for them (Katz, 2002; Bandura, 2010).

The very ability to transfer modes of thinking between pools of knowledge indicates that creative thinking can be taught, and that our students' toolbox can be practiced and widened. "Everyone's sky is the limit": the rise in the level of creativity is relative to the place every person is at any given moment, and there is no need to create an absolute measure or to compare between those who have a natural inclination to creativity to those who are unaware or untrained in creativity. One must think about coordinating reality, the age of the child, and their stage of development.

Surprisingly, it is the achievements of the digital era, in the context of creativity, that can be a barrier to creativity and innovation. Materials that exist on the net are too quickly available and provide instant gratification. The question is how to utilize the existing reality to suit the students and their needs, and only then can the digital world be advantageous.

If an educator can treat their search on the internet as brainstorming, then they can create something from something and turn it into something from nothing. The meaning is learning from what others have shared and creating something new from personal learning and planning. The "new" can also be a development or variation of existing tools that is suited to the students' needs and functions, and it might also help develop new ideas for tools or completely new ways. The ability to turn something that exists to "adapted new" is also the advantage of encouraging educational creativity that is born out of cooperation, fond emotions, and the power of teamwork.

In the context of adapted teaching, many teachers believe that the teaching of learning strategies is the domain of special education teachers. I say it belongs to everyone. It is the responsibility of the teacher to adapt their strategies, ways of teaching, methods, and means to the needs and style of each student. Creativity begins with learning how to think and how to adapt according to age and content. A teacher is obligated to be a lifelong learner, one who is constantly learning and adapting to the changing reality, one who thinks flexibly.

Examples for the use of creativity in education: the magic of connections

Interdisciplinarity, a celebration of education: The ability to connect between characteristics of one field of knowledge to another conceals within it great creativity. The connection creates something new that can be personal, collective, or cooperative. It can cover as wide a field or as narrow one as you decide. We can see this as leaving the familiar and daring to widen our minds. And then, as Dr. Seuss said: "Oh, the places you'll go."

In one of the schools I worked in, the ninth grade had a seemingly surprising interdisciplinary project: math and literature. Yes, it required cooperation and mutual learning from two faculties that seem to be from different worlds. However, the question was: Are they so different? The students learned the regular math curriculum. They also learned literature, respectively. Once a week, they had combined classes in which, as part of the process, the students learned to define and characterize elements, terms, and characteristics from both the math and the literature fields. They became familiar with artistic tools and learned, practiced, and improved skills of nonfiction writing. Later, the students were divided into groups to work on the final project: writing a children's book about a mathematical term or process. They were required to consistently plan, to have many discussions about their work, to submit a digest of their drafts to receive an evaluation on the process, to think with precision about the subject and storyline, and to connect terms from both fields. They learned to map concepts, define connections, and ask questions. They received guidance on graphic design for the final product. At the end of the year, together with the evaluation of the process, the students held an exhibit where the different groups presented their projects. The feeling of a celebration of education was felt throughout, and the students were proud of themselves and felt empowered by the educational staff.

Admit it: it is not uncommon to see that some students prefer the humanities while others prefer STEM, and those students often choose to neglect the other. The combination of literature and mathematics created new language and terminology. It did not stay at the level of comparison and analogy. It created something new: students reached a new mental level. The project calmed the anxieties of students who saw themselves only as humanities or STEM students, and highlighted the process and the final product. The division of roles and responsibilities among members of the groups allowed each student to express themselves and enabled a respectful and accepting discourse and a class and differential appraisal. I especially liked the projects in which the connections themselves created insights of acceptance and communication, social issues, and moral messages: noticing the loneliness of zero;

negative numbers with positive traits (for instance, two negatives result in a positive); and similar others. Even the teachers enjoyed a boost to their self-esteem and motivation because of the meaningful experience with their students and the success of the project.

Literary devices: the subject of literature, as well as Tanakh (Bible studies) and history, in this example, are subjects that rely on narrative and teach the student to engage with the creative thinking of the other: the author, the historian, the scribe of the Tanakh. The subjects focus on using tools of thought, analogy, connecting them, and upgrading them.

If we think for a moment about the essence of the **metaphor**, we will notice the creative connection between different unconnected words, where turning them into a phrase creates something new. The metaphor, as picturesque language, allows us to borrow characteristics from one field to another and create intention, a message, a hint of a constructed meaning. For instance, if we teach logic through familiar metaphors like "burning love" or "wildest dreams", if we anthropomorphize like in "listen to your heart", or if we use oxymorons where the contrast with the truth creates the effect like in "deafening silence" or "only choice", then we are teaching the students to think creatively. In the next stage, they will be required to create their own metaphors and present them. Thus, the combination of the **hint**, the Tanakh scripture connotation, of parallelism in the Tanakh verses, in different roles of completion, identicalness, contrast, as well as **giving life to characters** from history by creating a journal for them, a play based on them, correspondence with them, and more.

Creative linguistic adaptations: architecture and interior design for word families, verb and paradigm types, parts of speech, and more. If we can understand that grammar is a structured subject, that it has rules and a clear methodology, then we can make it accessible in a creative way using the field of architecture and interior design. Architecture and interior design, like grammar, is a precision-based methodological field that is spiced with imagination, innovation, and aesthetics.

For example, planning and constructing houses for **word families and conjugations**, constructing a community park with areas for verb and paradigm types, creating a **neighborhood of conjugations** where each conjugation is divided by tense and person, and so on. Using expressions from architecture and interior design such as design, color, texture, borders, and so on will give you, the educators, the stimulus to create the appropriate strategy for your students, will guide your path, and empower your students' experience and learning.

If we wish to adapt these ideas for preschoolers, when we teach the implications of phonology, we can build, using blocks or other tools, houses for word families in a more concrete and age-appropriate way. We could also partner opposites, rhymes, and synonyms in a rhyming ceremony, riddles with finger puppets, picture stories, or paralleling it to architectural plans.

Using detective riddles: investigating mysteries always invites divergent thinking while creating various scenarios and repeatedly proving or disproving them. I once taught writing skills to tenth-grade students. Many students are wary of writing for different reasons: style, developing a concept, linguistic precision, connectivity, structure, and more are all intimidating topics. Many of the students showed a gap between their ability to express themselves verbally versus on the written page. I got into the habit of starting each learning unit with a detective riddle on the topic we were about to address. The riddle was always connected to the writing exercise. I would set the stage as it would be if the detectives found it. The students were expected to ask yes/no questions. Anything answered with a yes would go on the board into a glossary map divided by categories, with a characterization of the connection between the terms such as: reminiscent of, similar to, opposite of, and contradicts. As we progressed, the students figured out both the mystery and the current class topic. From a glossary map, the plan grew and became the basis for the writing exercise and was an anchor that allowed students to cling to it when necessary.

Later, as I switched to teaching teachers and students of education, I would present this method using different subjects to investigate them in a data-based way, providing a 'soft entry' into any topic.

Example from Tanakh studies: **The story of Yael, the wife of Heber the Kenite, and the killing of Sisera**

The setting: Sisera is found dead in Yael's tent, obviously injured by a blunt instrument. What happened?

Type of questions to be asked (at the technique learning stage): How did he arrive at the tent and why? Who are the suspects and why? What was the murder instrument? (Many students will be familiar with the questions from the game Clue).

How to visually represent the clues:

Option A: A horizontal flow chart following the sequence of events with divergent connecting arrows to show the timeline.

Option B: A vertical timeline with the events with divergent arrows to explain the various connections.

In the digital age, you don't have to use a physical board. There are apps that allow one to create maps and charts, and these can be projected onto the board and used interactively.

Using arbitration methodology to promote creativity and encourage critical thinking: When I was a student, and even as a young teacher, one of the novel approaches was to have a courtroom in class: having students debate a dilemma or topic. The main advantage of the approach was that it gave the students the ability to see a topic in a new light, not through their own eyes but through a different perspective.

The world has changed. The dichotomous thinking of black and white, of the edges, is no longer popular. The reality is more complex, and people are more empathetic. The need, today, to account for many factors at once has grown, and the courts have a heavy caseload.

Over the years, people have become more moderate, more willing to see the full spectrum rather than simply the edges. The softer skills are becoming more important and prominent—and not only lawyers can become arbitrators.

The main advantage of these methods is that they rely on structured techniques, flexibility, and communication that is appraising and compromising. In the adult world, formal education and training are required to be an arbitrator. However, the techniques and principles that are the core of the idea can be implemented in class in different subjects. Training students to the aforementioned method encourages flexible thinking, a main element of creativity; empathetic communication; learning to look and listen before you leap to conclusions; learning to compare and contrast, to categorize, to notice pluses and minuses; and learning to create new creative solutions. Solutions that are compromises or win-win situations when possible. Even disagreeing can be the result of a creative process because it invites the process of arbitration that initiates creative thinking.

Now you can take your subject, consult your colleagues, exchange ideas, and create your own win-win scenario.

One of the professional courses I took over the years (a teacher should constantly be learning) was an arbitration course. You can use the six basic principles of the arbitration process to create a structure that can be used in any subject. Here are the steps and principles that provide the basic structure:

SO, WHAT IS ARBITRATION?

The process of creating a bridge between two sides or more that are in conflict and bringing them to an agreement.

Six steps of arbitration:

1. **Preparation:** this stage includes the opening statement of the arbitrator defining the issue, the goals of the process, and the rules governing it.
2. **The two sides present the issue:** the opening statements of the two conflicting sides. The sides present the issue and dilemmas.
3. **Identifying and understanding the claims of both sides:** A discussion in which the arbitrator encourages each side to answer the opening claims of the other side.
4. **Private meetings with the arbitrator:** each side will meet individually with the arbitrator to examine their needs and desires and find an acceptable solution for the conflict.
5. **Creating solution options by negotiating:** the arbitrator brings both sides back together for a joint negotiation.
6. **Coming to and formulating an agreement**

Principles in putting the arbitration process into practice:[4]

- Separating the man from the problem: neutralizing emotions

---

4   Nishri,N. (2018), 8 Principles of arbitration you can practice yourself ; retrieved May 2020 https://www.ynet.co.il/articles/0,7340,L-5262336,00.html

- "Know where you came from and where you are going": planning and definitions
- What guides you? Taking a step back to analyze the issue and the perspectives surrounding it
- Know where the other side is headed: which goals and claims lead the different sides in the discussion
- Sometimes you can just stop: inhibition, active and empathetic listening, word choice
- If you want a good answer, ask an excellent question: asking leading questions
- Write, write: documenting what the other side says for restraint and planning the next stage
- Go slow to go fast: decision-making takes time.

Example of adaptive behavior using creative thinking, case study: True case, names have been changed

Steve was a student of mine from seventh to twelfth grade. He was a bright student diagnosed with severe Combined Presentation of Attention Deficit Hyperactivity Disorder (ADHD) including specific learning disorders. Sharon was socially popular and had a good sense of rhythm and great love of music (remember mapping strengths from the previous chapter?). He sat alone at a desk designed for two and, during class, would drum on the table. The other students complained the noise was distracting but feared insulting him. I noticed that in classes when he drummed, he was completely attentive in class, cooperating and learning the lesson. In classes when he was not allowed to drum, he couldn't learn, which showed that drumming was a facilitator of attention rather than a naughty behavior. Analyzing all the data made me ask, what would give the class the required silence but would not rob Sharon of the ability to drum and learn? The answer turned out to be simple: I brought an old pillow from home and, together with the handyman, attached it to the side of Sharon's desk. He could now drum silently and not bother the class. Win-win.

In conclusion, it is both small and large inventions such as entrepreneurship, project-based learning, hackathons, cooperative learning, and techniques that combine the goals of education with modern reality, with adapting thinking instruments, and with your creativity that will promote creativity among your students. Yes, you, educators, architects of the brain, have this power. Very quickly you can see how the students become young entrepreneurs even with your teaching materials.

Win-win, we said?

CHAPTER 6

ADAPTIVE EVALUATION

From the early stages of development, people will face constant verbal and nonverbal evaluations so long as there is an evaluator and someone evaluated. In the last few decades, the attitude toward evaluation and its definitions has changed a lot. This change is also evident in educational evaluation.

In our area, there are four main complaints used to criticize standard, static, psychometric, comparative, and "objective":

1. Conventional tests may discriminate against certain groups in society. Due to social and environmental circumstances, these groups often do not perform as well as other groups; alternatively, they may have skills not assessed using standardized testing. Thus, they experience a social tax of sorts.
2. The tests do not evaluate valuable characteristics such as creativity, motivation, values, social adaptivity, and personality traits. These traits contribute to cognitive function just as much as the "pure" cognitive skills.
3. Standardized testing focuses on the final result of brain activities and ignores processes of thinking and learning. However, it is important to understand the learning processes in order to use them in educational interventions aimed at cognitive modification.

4. Standardized testing does not reveal specific difficulties: difficulties that slow down learning. It, therefore, does not enable processes and interventions that help the student grow (Tzuriel, 1998, 1999).

If we put aside the upcoming reforms, we should still ask ourselves what adaptive evaluation methods are. Note, I'm not talking specifically about testing methods. However, testing methods can be included, at least until tenth grade, when the formal requirement for the *Bagrut* tests (Israeli matriculation), which are still part of the comparison-based psychometric method, begins.

The ability of the educator to evaluate their students is essential. The feedback they give them is influential and possibly invaluable to their self-esteem and self-confidence, two factors that affect their daily life and future. We must understand that we do not evaluate merely because it is a requirement of the educational system. For this reason, the perception of the educator as an evaluator is a whole world of knowledge and thought.

The discussion over systematic educated evaluation of the achievements of students in Israel has grown, in Israel, since the Dovrat Committee (2003) that highlighted the importance of evaluation in the education system, and since the establishment of the National Authority of Measurement and Evaluation (*Hareshut Haartzit Lemedida veHa'aracha*—RAMH) (Levin-Rozalis, 2012).

As the new millennium approached, the education system in Israel began to formally acknowledge the central importance of educational evaluation processes in advancing students' achievements (Dressler, 2005). Later, in 2006, the RAMH was established, the National Authority of Measurement and Evaluation, an independent body responsible for all the educational evaluation activities in Israel. One of its central values is the concept of "measurement in the service of learning": a combination of **internal and external summative evaluations**, to measure and rank, with formative evaluation, to promote learning and assist with education processes (Levin-Rozalis & Lapidot, 2009).

Levi-Vered (2013) discusses the connection between educators' self-efficacy and their perception of themselves as evaluators versus their expertise in evaluation. She presents findings that teachers who have low self-efficacy regarding measurement and educational evaluation also have a negative perception of evaluation and vice versa. She adds that a high perception of one's self-efficacy concerning evaluation is connected to seeing evaluation as a useful and relevant tool. The number of years of experience an educator has does not seem to matter either way.

Thus, naturally and historically, the purpose of the evaluation in education is to examine the amount of knowledge and skills the students learned in class and the student's achievements vis a vis their classmates. The evaluator is, usually, the teacher. The evaluation results help them determine the obvious steps for improving educational achievements (Erlisch, 2008; Nevo, 2003).

The connection between acts of evaluation and perceptions of education and learning is very much one that combines and merges all the pedagogical actions, including evaluation of student behavior and achievement. It is influenced, as we said, by the educator's perception of the act of educating, the process and goals of the evaluation, and the essence of learning (Levi-Vered, 2013). These connections raise questions concerning the objective of the evaluation, knowledge, taxonomy of thinking processes, processes of learning, functions of behavior, emotions, society, creativity, and more.

In the last few years, other Israeli organizations, including the umbrella organizations of all the educators in Israel (regardless of student age), have begun encouraging teachers at both school and preschool, as well as education-adjacent professions, to join educational programs that see **"the educator as a researcher"**. These programs see the researcher as part of the process that assists them in prioritizing educational goals and giving valuable feedback to the students. Several of the organizations reward teachers who join continuing education programs of this ilk with better salaries and promotions. The purpose of the continuing education programs in this field is twofold: (1) develop the expertise of educators in researching questions from their daily work. (2) Enrich their academic knowledge in the relevant topics while publishing their results and findings and cooperating with colleagues and professional communities.

The methodological emphasis is on creating spiral-like processes of examining the current situation, modifying it, evaluating it, re-modifying it accordingly, reevaluating it, and creating a differential evaluation.

Other questions that repeatedly arise concern the perceptual paradigm of the evaluation goal as formative or summative. A formative evaluation takes place during learning and is used, most commonly, to evaluate the learning processes and is performed **for learning**. A summative evaluation takes place at the end of the learning process or the end of certain stages within it. It evaluates the achievements of the student and their command of the knowledge and skills learned, meaning **it evaluates the learning**. The adaptive evaluation method, which is essentially evaluation in motion, is a dynamic evaluation that combines the two paradigms in an advanced dialogue between the goals of "before-during-after."

The first question we must always ask ourselves is what the goal of the evaluation is. According to the goal, we will choose the method. For many years we grouped all the evaluation tools that are not comparison-based or numeric under the name 'alternative evaluation.' I am not disparaging this name because under certain circumstances it was necessary. I am, however, challenging it in our current reality of changing circumstances. The evaluation, in my opinion, is not an alternative to anything. It exists and has a role. Moreover, every evaluation event is assumed to have an achievable goal. Therefore, who is to say that all students and all skills should be evaluated by the same method or tools? As long as the same goal is achieved?

In preparation for every evaluation event, we must ask ourselves: **Why** are we evaluating? **What** do we want to discover? And, **how** are we going to complete our goal? We will quickly find out that if we intend to evaluate the students, compared to what they have already achieved, and obtain the image that is most true to reality regarding each student and the performance they have exhibited in a way that reflects their learning, we will have to do adaptive manipulation on the source that we prepare as an evaluation platform, to create indicators that allow us to list the goals of the evaluation and turn them into adaptive behavioral goals and define our expectations to the student. We must remember, every evaluation of a final product is preceded by a process that determines its design. We should also evaluate the process and the steps in between.

Examples of formative adaptive evaluation:

As we said, a formative evaluation is evaluating the processes. Mostly, it is continuous or invites continuity from its characterization as a feedback-based evaluation: one that includes a dialogue between the evaluator and the one being evaluated. As such, the decision whether to perform it independently or through a dialogue with the student is the teacher's decision, based on their goals. I will now present three ways to perform a formative evaluation. The variations on these methods and others are adaptations to the unique needs and abilities of your students.

Evaluation of knowledge, levels of thinking and skills/learning processes/various functions:

Digest (portfolio) - expresses the perception that the process of evaluation is integral to learning: a continuing process that documents the development of abilities over time. The purpose of the digest is to show evaluation for learning.

It is, in fact, a collection of the results of the student that are presented via repeated drafts and using dialogue at set points, or, as a final product that is collected as evidence of the learning process that occurred, the achievements, advancement, knowledge, and abilities of the student. Creating the digest is performed with the student actively participating in the content creation, the selection criteria for what goes into the digest, and the metacognitive reflection of the student. They are evaluated using clear indicators that include preselected criteria to judge the learning activities and content.

Today, you can see the use of digests in a way that is aimed at elements of the evaluation and is part of the Bagrut grade: 30% or more of the final grade. It can also be an alternative for a final product grade in any field and subject. The adaptation to age is performed according to the educator's goals; thus, it is flexible in how it defines the content, skills, gradual development, various functions, and more. Many examples of types of indicators can be seen on the website of Menucha Birenbaum *Behavanaya Matmedet.*

Reflection diary - metacognitive pedagogy:

Many educators have already encountered the word reflection, but its meanings are varied.
This makes sense since the goals of reflection define its content. Thus, the identity of the person performing reflection also changes. Reflection can be carried out by a student, a group, an educator, or a whole staff.

The essence of reflection is thinking about our actions, what motivates our actions, and our decisions. It is a process of thinking that occurs as an internal dialogue, the purpose of which is to produce personal meaning and upgrade our goals in the future while documenting the inner dialogue between the earlier knowledge and the newer one. Reflection embodies the ability of the writer to look into oneself in order to notice and evaluate in an intelligent but noncritical manner the processes of learning. As such, it serves as an invaluable tool to promote learning and teaching.

Example of a reflection diary of a student (MS) in a course about cognitive modification: The students were asked to do structured metacognitive reflection after each class and presented a sample digest for evaluation. The indicators for the evaluation included identifying previous vs. new knowledge, representing the learned material using charts, representing thoughts: "How is knowledge represented inside my head?" identifying elements of the class that were understood or not, and declaring an interest and needs to enhance learning later on.

This tool also represents "know where you're coming from and to where you are going" and includes the students in the responsibility of navigating their learning. As you can see, the diary is presented as authentically as possible.

9.11 REFLECTION DIARY

1. New Terminology

Transcendence - beyond something
Internal representation - creating an internal representation requires translating the elements of the problem or action from their original form to a different one . The internal representation of the goal is like a series of situations that can lead it from the original situation of the problem to the end situation, the solution itself.

2. Earlier terms that were clarified

Cognition - mind, consciousness, describes human knowledge. The term consciousness refers to knowledge or information that exists in a person. It also includes the processes of acquiring knowledge, processing it, and putting it into practice. Additionally, it describes the instrument or the "organ"—the brain, the human mind—in which the processes of human knowledge happen.

Cognitive psychology - subfield of psychology, deals with the way human consciousness functions and knowledge is processed inside our brain into representation and meaning.

The mental processes by which the information is processed: distal stimulus<perception<cognitive processing< high-level mental functions.

"Processes" - the fact of improving different characteristics to make a whole image with some meaning, like writing utensils. In this process, there are: time, neurotransmission, and the quality of the product that is affected by the quality of the process. You need to be careful not to implement mistakes because it is difficult, afterwards, to uproot them.

"Representation" - the way this improvement is expressed in the consciousness and remains in it in the form of a memory, what we see in our mind's eye when someone says, "writing utensils."

The term **Concept** - the term refers, roughly, to joint characteristics that are used to group certain elements in a category, like a folder: a general definition and ideas and words connected to that term. In fact, the internal definitions are contained in the concept.

3. **Structure of the lesson:**

Here are the subjects that came up during the lesson. Each term in the chart came with an example in the classroom that clarified it.

```
┌─────────────────────────────┐
│   Cognitive Psychology      │
└─────────────────────────────┘
              │
              ▼
┌─────────────────────────────────┐
│ Deals with: processing knowledge into │
│    meaning and representation   │
└─────────────────────────────────┘

        ┌─────────────┐
        │ Sensory input │
        └─────────────┘
              │
              ▼
        ┌─────────────┐
        │ Perception  │
        └─────────────┘
              │
              ▼
        ┌─────────────┐
        │ Processing  │
        └─────────────┘
              ┊
              ┊
              ▼
```

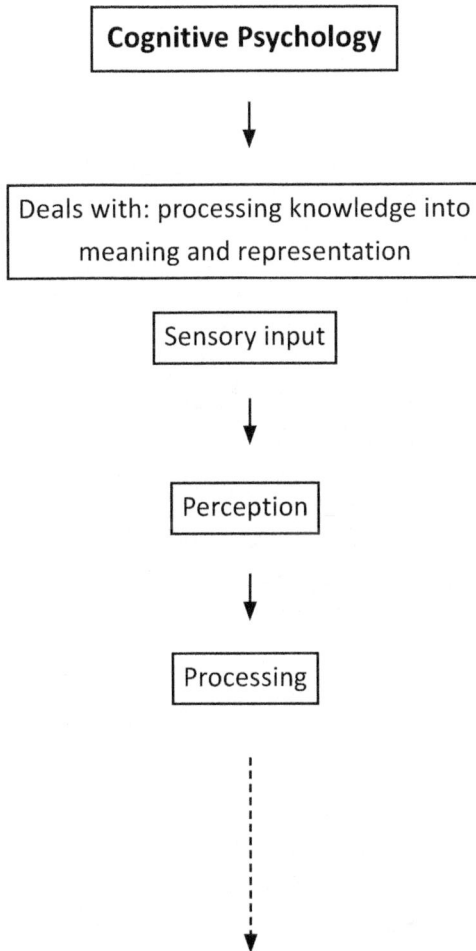

Improving the characteristics is
done by two skills of thinking:
- *Distinction*
- *Generalization}*

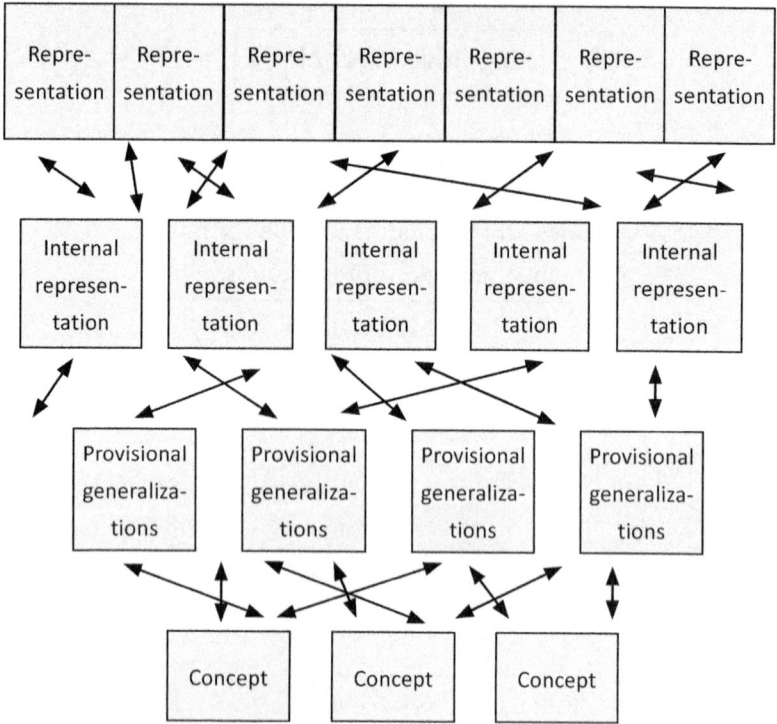

There is a need to develop the differences between the terms internal representation and representation. Additionally, I feel a need to increase my understanding of the process that people go through who have different cognitive abilities until the concept is created.

28.12 REFLECTION DIARY

1. New Terminology:

Modality

2. Earlier terms that were clarified:

Dynamic assessment - a sampling of the cognitive structural modifiability

Dynamic evaluation is an assessment of the ability to learn based on the assumption that the visible level of functionality of the individual does not necessarily reflect their ability.

Statistical assessment- the standardized test

3. Structure of the lesson:

PART 1: THEORY
Stages of assessment

- Pre-test, no intervention
- Learning, mediator
- Post-test, testing for generalization and transference as well
- Levels of intervention
- Pre-test
- Intervention

The seven cognitive dimensions		

Content	Commu-nication modality	Intel-lectual modality}				

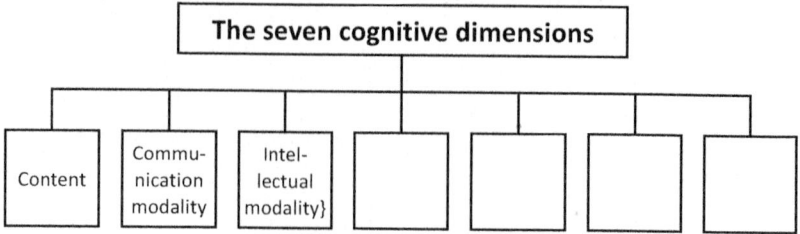

	Input	Processing	Output
Battery - a unit within the assessment that examines cognitive modality, the cognitive aspect (divided into sub-tasks)			

PART 2: TRYING OUT DYNAMIC ASSESSMENT - REY'S VISUAL COMPLEX FIGURE

<u>Assessment has five stages:</u>

- In this stage we copied a complex shape -
  PRE-TEST COPYING
- In this stage we tried to recreate the complex shape -
  PRE-TEST MEMORY
- In this stage we learned to organize the shape through mediation -
  MEDIATION (LEARNING)
- In this stage we copied the shape while working in an organized fashion and using the tools we learned -
  POST-TEST COPYING

- In this stage we recreated the shape while implementing the learning done -
POST-TEST MEMORY

There is a need for a deeper understanding of analyzing the evaluation. Additionally, it's not clear to me which modalities were assessed in the dynamic assessment we went through.

Transference from a qualitative assessment to a quantitative one:

A significant portion of the image of an educator as a researcher in motion is the impressions and insights they gain as they and the student do their work. However, lack of ability with attention can naturally be seen, interpreted, and extrapolated into responses and an evaluation. From these results, we learn that different viewpoints give us different impressions. Because of this, the collection of qualitative data must be processed methodologically to understand the scope of the phenomenon, as well as its impact and the skills it contains. One of the methods I use is "event recording": this is methodological documentation that marks and counts skills such as social, behavioral, learning, etc. Only at the end of the process do we summarize and draw conclusions for the future. This can be done using direct observation, an external observer, documented observation, and, given permission, filming and analyzing upon review. It can also be done by the student themselves as a form of self-assessment, after teaching them the appropriate rating scale, mostly for short-term goals and behavior reflection.

Example of an observation chart (daily observation aimed at recording social events):

The following example is taken from the work of A.P. (under my supervision). Here, she documented two situations: class and recess. She assessed predetermined social behaviors: before and after the program to include children with autism began. The option of collecting data from different observations at different times and including reactions to interventions gives us more than the result; it gives us, predominantly, an understanding of the effect adjusting and adapting goals has in addition to assisting us in evaluating progress.

Appendix 2:

Name of student:_____

Group:_____**Number in study:**_____

Time ╱ Behavior	Before inclusion class	Before inclusion recess	After inclusion class	After inclusion recess
Creates connections with new friends				
Talks to friends while sitting down				
Participates in class and answers questions				
Hangs out and plays with friends during recess				
Comes to class with equipment				
Eats politely				
Eats alone or with friends				
Is violent with others				
Cries, yells, hits themselves, throws things				
Asks correctly to go to the bathroom				
Uses words as a gesture (thanks, sorry, goodbye, etc.)				

Examples for a summative adaptive evaluation:

As mentioned, a summative evaluation happens at the end of the learning process or the end of stages within the learning process. It usually serves as an evaluation of the student's achievements and control of the skills and knowledge acquired. Meaning, this is a tool for **evaluating the learning** or general functions.

At this stage, adaptive evaluation means adaptive to the strengths, abilities, and clear styles of the student. It is differential in the sense of a single purpose and unified instructions, but is open to a variety of products, tools, or unique adaptive products. The indicator for the type of evaluation, just like creating the final product itself, can be personal or collective; it can be created by the educator alone or, preferably, together with the student.

For example, evaluating the knowledge acquired about the Dreyfus Affair, after it was studied in class:

Representations in writing or drawing: test, quiz, paper; comic strip, caricature, informational pamphlet, position paper, writing trial summaries for the defense and the prosecution, a lawyer's opinion, representation of the case in a connecting chart, writing a screenplay, a skit, a song, the place of the media person and art, building a board game, a track, cards, and more.

Standing in front of the class, teacher, audience: a play, simulation, puppet or shadow theatre, slideshow, Hyde Park style speech, pantomime, billboards with direct messages or positive propaganda, street performances, and more.

Audio representations and digital media: composing and performing a song on the subject or making up new lyrics to a familiar and beloved tune, editing a short video that contains all the information, creating a representative digital collage, creating a PowerPoint with recorded audio, interactive quizzes incorporated in a slideshow, and more.

Encouraging independent studies with the evaluation: the evaluation is a trust-building element. Like self-criticism, monitoring and feedback, it is a life skill. Many times, we tend to be the ones who give external feedback, the ones who write notes and grades, draw a smiley face, and give verbal feedback while requiring corrections or verbal praise, and this too has rules. However, we must remember that in order to combine, depending on the age and the goal, evaluation with self-criticism, even if it sometimes means that one needs to correct or readjust their actions/work, just like in life. We can always use our feedback using the correct adapted strengths of the evaluation activity.

Examples of internal monitoring and feedback:

Using multiple-choice questions:

Representing the correct answers using different letters and all the letters together form a word of praise, upgrades: representing a series of numbers that are a code for an escape pod or using shapes, signs, and symbols that form a riddle.

Mazes with correct/incorrect answers in the middle that help one reach the end; yes/no questions, with or without explanations, and checking them in pairs using a key.

Cloze exercises, with or without a word chest, with the words hiding under a scratch surface (like on a lottery ticket).

Checking the test using a transparency sheet on a page that has been solved; checking oneself using an answers key.

With young children: connecting dots, a string of numbers, coloring according to a legend of colors and shapes, completing a puzzle, visual matching games such as the Memory Game, picture lottery, and so on. Higher levels for the extra fast, ambitious, and advanced can be achieved by the need to solve the previous level to get to the next one, each level contains clues for the next level, or you follow a roadmap of sorts.

Open tasks: peer assessment according to predetermined criteria and learning how to provide feedback, exchanging questions and riddles written by the students and checking them, answer bingo for questions presented to all, and more.

Tracking task performance

The same reasons that encourage the self-critical independent learner are the reasons I usually recommend creating means for assessing advancement by the learner. This way, they accumulate successes and eventually progress. This can be done using digital means such as marking it on an Excel sheet, on a table, or by any other means, and it can be done using reflection or by tools that are connected to concepts and shape the learning environment. For instance, using a personal fake passport in Geography or marking points on a map, using a punch card in a subject, a travel journal, a themed notebook, and anything else you can think about.

At the same time, it is recommended that the teacher keep records as well so that the student always has a backup. My recommendation is to use a digital or manual table that contains the names of the students and the topic units learned and that uses a color-coded legend to represent each child's level of knowledge in each subject. The representation via color helps us notice weak points and strong ones and adapt our methodology accordingly.

Example of differential monitoring (online):

	Yeki	Gadi	Ruti	Tzviya	Nofar	Sapir	Or
Subtracting with extending the length and converting numbers	●	●	●	●	●	●	○
Subtraction with numbers 1-10	●	●	●	●	●	●	○
Counting backwards	●	●	●	●	●	●	○
Addition with breaking down numbers by ten	●	●	●	●	●	●	○
Addition with numbers 11-20	●	○	○	●	●	○	○
Learning commutative properties	●	○	○	○	○	○	○
Addition with numbers 1-10 Unidirectional	○	○	○	○	○	○	○

LEGEND: ● 0-50 ● 51-60 ● 61-75 ○ 75-100

CHAPTER 7

ADAPTIVE TEACHING FOR EMOTIONAL AND SOCIAL NEEDS

"A teacher affects eternity; he can never tell where his influence stops."

(Henry Brooks Adams)

The saying "Every child needs one adult who will believe in him, listen to him, and help him find his path" might be seen as a cliché. However, every cliché holds a kernel of truth: every cliché comes out of insights from real life.

In the last few years, the discussion about Social and Emotional Learning (SEL) has taken the front and center place in the field of education. SEL is hardly new and has always been important. However, with the coming of the new decade, a decade which requires adapted definitions for the image of the adult and their functions rather than knowledge in a specific field, SEL is claiming its rightful place. The understanding that this element is part of the backbone of education, part of the inherent values of education, changes its image from a passing educational fashion.

Shadmi (2019)[5] writes: "Social and Emotional Learning is pri-

---

5   Shadmi, H. (2019) Lemida chevratit-rigshit vepsichopedagogia [Social-emotional learning and psycho-pedagogy]; Bitaon Machon Mofet https://bitaon.macam.ac.il/articles/11446

marily an approach that sees people as a whole including a body, a soul, a mind, emotions, and a social life; this is a perception that sees teaching, learning, the classroom program as a social group. It sees the connection between school and family as spaces for development, empowerment, and advancement of emotional welfare of all the participants."

Osher et al. (2016)[6] quote Elias et al. regarding the definition of Social and Emotional Learning (SEL). They define it as "the processes by which children and adults acquire and apply core competencies to recognize and manage emotions, set and achieve positive goals, appreciate the perspectives of others, establish and maintain supportive relationships, make responsible decisions, and handle personal and interpersonal situations constructively."

As previously mentioned, working with social and emotional learning is not purely about its essence: it is about the connection between SEL and situations that society and the individual face in a changing and adapting reality. As such, SEL requires us to practice, implement, and be consistent in our psycho-pedagogical view of social groups and the individuals within them.

It has been many years now but, still, many educators think that the social and emotional care of the students is the role of school counselors. The result is that not all the students are accessible all the time, especially in real-time. The understanding that a teacher can see themselves as "a whole person with a body, soul, mind, emotion, and social life" forces us to see our students the way they see themselves in their daily life. SEL is part of our moral obligation

---

6   Osher, D., Kidron, Y., Brackett, M., Dymnicki, A., Jones, S., & Weissberg, R. P. (2016) Advancing the science and practice of social and emotional learning: Looking back and moving forward. *Review of Research in Education 40*(1), 644-681

and our responsibility for the welfare of our students.

Various reports from employers, and even the OECD, focus on the image of the alumnus seeking a job or higher education in the third decade of the 21st century. Almost all these reports emphasize the importance of soft skills as a key to an independent, developing, efficient, and advancing alumnus. Soft skills are skills, strengths, and characteristics that aren't directly related to professional training but set the alumnus apart from the crowd. Many studies show that soft skills predict success in school, work, and life in general. These skills include, among others, emotional intelligence, communication patterns with others, the ability to present and solve problems, persuasion, creativity, handling stressful situations, ability to negotiate, team cooperation, leadership skills, adaptability to change, and persistence. All these skills can be taught, improved, and increased in students. They can also provide the base for creating goals that help create educational working plans.

It is common to discuss life skills, the independent learner, a beneficial educational climate, accepting the other, and other concepts that are part of the humanistic discourse that characterizes the modern era. However, the underlying assumption of this book is that each individual is a unique other, and, as such, they experience things in ways both similar and different from others through their own reality lens that includes much more than the school itinerary.

A meta-analysis of the research material completed by Goldberg et al. (2019)[7] shows that children and teenagers who attend SEL programs improve their ability to use soft skills. The programs also improve their attitude toward themselves, others, and institutions. Additionally, the programs promote students' prosocial behavior; thus, they enjoy a sense of psychological relief and improved academic achievements.

Therefore, it is appropriate that the educational profession, the example it sets, and its applications include an overhead view of the educator, and a constant evaluation of the social and emotional compass of groups and individuals; meaning monitoring the social-emotional pulse daily. One should make space and time for discourse on the subject, practicing strategies, implementing insights, both for the group and the individual: taking a step back to move forward.

As we will see later on, the central interface between the profile of the alumnus and the functions of the learner occurs in the interpersonal field: social and communication patterns, and in the personal field: emotional, reflective, meta-cognitive. It justifies adapting teaching and learning to the development of these fields at any age and any interaction with content and skills. It is difficult in our daily lives to separate the behavioral interaction of the two fields. However, in learning, you can create personal and interpersonal goals and practice them together and apart.

---

7   Goldberg, J. M., Sklad, M., Elfrink, T. R., Schreurs, K. M., Bohlmeijer, E. T., & Clarke, A. M (2019). Effectiveness of interventions adopting a whole school approach to enhancing social and emotional development: a meta-analysis. *European Journal of psychology of Education*, *34*(4), 755-782

OVERHEAD VIEW AND STATUS ASSESSMENT:

The web is filled with questionnaires that allow different ages of children and adults to examine their social positioning and emotions. However, one of the best tools I've found for understanding and mapping the emotional and social situation in groups that applies to all ages is called "Where am I in this situation?"

So, where am I in this situation?

You are the star. Mark the square that best describes you in relation to your class. **Give** it a name and answer the following questions.

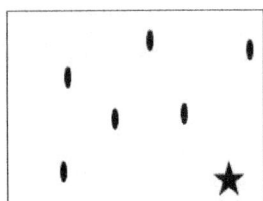

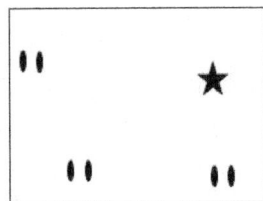

The questions:
1. Who do you want to sit next to?
2. Who would you like to work with in the group?
3. What can you contribute to the group?
4. What would you like to learn from the group?

Mapping the data:

Name:	Rejected/ isolated	The center of attention	One out of a non-inclu-sionary group	One vs. the cliques	Answers to questions
Eyal	X				1. Gadi 2. Tamar 3.Read quickly 4. To cooperate
Gadi					
Noa					
Tamar					

Think for a moment:

How much information did you get from such a simple mapping?

Of course, you could decide to go even further and create a socio-gram; you could find and color different and shared choices; you could make educated decisions on how to plan and build groups for different purposes; arrange the students' seating; give out roles; and other educational and social aspects that will advance the individual and the group. If you give out the same exercise in the middle of the year and the end of it, you will be able to determine if the decisions you made were correct and decide whether to con-tinue as you are or to change your program.

Another moment of psycho-pedagogy:

Psycho-pedagogy, as we said, is a view that emphasizes aware-ness of awakening feelings and viewpoints that are formed within relationships that develop in the teaching-learning processes (The Ministry of Education, 2014).[8] According to this view, it is the responsibility of the educator to turn and focus their attention to the emotions that awaken in the processes of teaching and learning, to determine the positions and views of themselves and their students while constantly examining whether these processes are advancing or slowing down.

"The ethical perception of caring sees education as a practice of relationships that exist on the basis of natural caring, love, compassion, generosity, and attention, that is directly related to the processes of teaching and learning" (The Ministry of Education, 2014).

Social and communication exercise:

One of the things we all know as adults who belong to teams and different social groups is that being friendly does not mean being friends. Belonging to a social group is first and foremost a human need, a need with characteristics and elements that change according to one's age, situation, and goals. The understanding that learning happens within interactions and relationships contains within it the quality of the connection between teachers and students, the support of the educators for the feeling of belonging, the ability, and autonomy of the students. This understanding focuses the student on realizing the connection between their opinions on the educational climate and their views on their own functions, learning modalities, and academic achievements.

---

8   The Ministry of Education (2014), **Psifas: psicho-pedagogia - moodaut veyediaa bemelechet hachinuch vehahoraa [Mosaic: Psychopedagogy - awareness and knowing in the art of education and teaching]**

In the beginning, the work on social communication is connected to an active and meaningful understanding of several basic elements and their practice. In my opinion, first and foremost, you should focus on the concept of **responsibility to MMMO**:

Me, myself, and I
My family, my siblings
My social circle, my friends
Others, society in general

As it stands, you can develop and widen the meanings of the sub-concepts: personal responsibility, mutual responsibility, general social responsibility. From here, we can and should transfer and generalize the concept to different parts of life such as cooperation, environmental responsibility, and more.

When a student internalizes their responsibility as an able and present person in the world, they become empowered and willing to act independently because "this is worthy, this does me good, and not because I need this."

Another model I used to use to flexibly guide myself, one that was born out of adapting to the creation of adaptive social programs for the group, is the **SCRAP model**:

S self & social awareness, self-confidence, sharing
C communication, collectivism, connections
R roles, reflection
A asking for help, accepting help, accepting others, attention
P peer assessment, participation, perception of society and oneself in it

As the model is general, it encourages creating an adaptable program, adaptable by age, population, needs of the group, and social positions. I, like many educators, tend to hoard examples. As such, I used to collect and create activities for each category and use them appropriately.

One of the better tools I acquired from Eyal Shani, a student of mine and long-time teacher, was intended to work on cooperation by building communication patterns, transferring roles, listening to others, and participating.

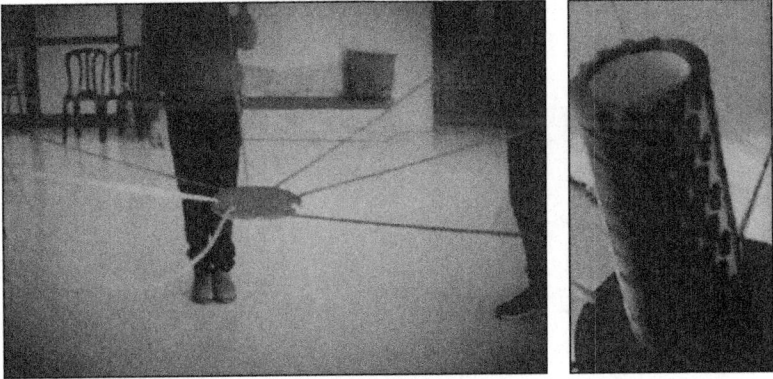

Credit: Eyal Shani: e.shani100@gmail.com

It is a tool that can be given different names, created easily, and used on various occasions. It invites teamwork, coordination, and adapting the rules and difficulty level of the game according to age and goals.

In a small group, you could use different colored ropes to represent different roles and belongings.

Eyal's rationale and insight:

- ☑ The tool is used to practice and improve communication abilities and social interaction between the students. To succeed in the mission, the students must cooperate wholly so that a utensil can stay in the air and doesn't fall off the surface.
- ☑ The tool reinforces the student's ability to listen and concentrate as well as their persistence while weakening impulsive behavior.

Goals can change according to the group, goals, and needs. For instance, (and I say this affectionately) Eyal wrote goals and rules appropriate to his group. His rationale for the game matches his group's characteristics and needs (confidentiality prohibits me from revealing more information).

Goals for the learner's functions:

- Practicing and the ability of students to cooperate and work in tandem with their classmates
- Creating social situations that require attention to the other in the group
- Strengthening communication and verbal abilities thereby creating an interpersonal interaction between the class students.

Goals for content:

- Improving the students' fine motor skills
- Improving coordination
- Improving persistence in tasks

Instruction for use of the tool with a utensil on a surface in the center of the specific group:

☑ Choose a task manager to give the instructions to the rest of the group. It can be any of the participants or a staff member.

☑ The task manager asks the participants to stand in a circle around the group challenge. Participants are spaced equally apart / every student stands in front of a rope.

☑ The task manager instructs the group to hold and pull the ropes carefully in tandem so that the utensil on the central surface will be stable and not fall.

☑ When each of the ropes is equally tight, and the utensil is balanced on the surface in the air, the task manager tells the participants to move to another location of their choice.

☑ The participants need to move to the new location chosen by the task manager without dropping the utensil in the center.

☑ Once they arrive at the new location, the task manager gives the instruction to lower the surface in the middle until it touches the floor.

Here are several other examples—activities aimed at increasing cooperation—that are appropriate for any age and use either writing or images. The activities can be held in either regular classes, using material from them, or during classes specifically aimed at social skills:

Puzzle - create a poster with a message. On one side, you have a task. On the other side, there is an internal evaluation of the message that you created from elements of tasks you gave to the groups. Variation: dominos or matching games.

Treasure Hunt in class or the schoolyard. Yes, the same game we played as children with early preparation of clues in the classroom, schoolyard, or under students' chairs. A free digital version of the game can be found online in: "Treasure Hit".

Escape rooms: activities that require cooperation to find clues and codes that lead to the answer.

Team Story game: every student adds a word or a sentence to the previous student's work. Together, they create a whole statement/story. Works as an activity to summarize a class or as a rehearsal before evaluation

Social backpack: individually or in a group, create a regular ritual to open or close the day. A ritual that imprints the group with the social insights of that day, thus creating a weekly social reflective summary. It can be made as a mobile backpack, virtual backpack, or a changing board on the classroom walls.

Friendship sun: a tool used during recess; one I saw in several schools. Every grade appoints students to be sun monitors. The sun monitor stands inside a friendship sun drawn in the middle of the schoolyard. The monitor changes daily, weekly, or monthly. Their job is to identify students who are alone during recess and invite them to play (remember? You don't have to be friends to practice friendship). Reports from schools that used this method show that this exercise can empower the appointed sun monitor as well as socially insecure children or those who lack the social skills to connect and belong.

The truth on the back: a tool that encourages peer review, unlike the examples given in adaptive evaluation, reflection, and social contract. Remember the activity where we would connect a page to the back of every participant and write positive things about them? This tool includes an internal circle and an external one. The movement of one of the circles is clockwise, and the Truth on the Back is an action that every time it is repeated, at different times, the educator or the group chooses what they write. It can include positive traits, advice for improvement, and more. The main rules of the group social contract are: you can't use the word "no" and you can only make positive helpful statements. There is no need to write the author's name, and it is desirable to process together with the way the person receiving the advice perceives and feels about what was written to them.

Of course, many other activities can be adapted as well as various tools. However, if you have found in this list some direction and inspiration that allows you to plan and be creative, flexible, and sensitive, then it is all the better for it.

EMOTIONAL REFLECTIVE METACOGNITIVE EXERCISES:

The educational space invites constant management of emotions toward oneself as well as toward the other. This is true regardless of the age, personality, and location of the student. It includes inner reflection on aspects from the routine and changing reality, from times of pressure and stress, on the personal level and the larger scale: national security crises, pandemics, and so on. One's resilience, i.e. psychological durability, changes from person to person and includes fundamental personality traits, previous experience, and education. Of course, there needs to be a distinction between therapy and education. If a student reacts inappropriately to situations, they need to be directed to the appropriate places to be diagnosed and treated. However, many educational activities can improve the individual's ability to withstand and handle complex and varied emotional situations.

The educational approach contains a large number of skills known as life skills. You can find many programs online aimed at different ages and different values contained under that name. However, we can discuss several basic elements that can be used in education regularly without the need to select a specific program.

One of my favorite programs[9] is the BEAMS program, because it can be used in modular fashion and its sections can be adapted to different goals and needs. It is based around five elements:

---

9   The Ministry of Education. (2009), "on b"e" - hatfisa haholistit shel kishurei chayim [On Be - the holistic perception of life skills] https://meyda.education.gov.il/files/shefi/KishureyChayimCatab/onbilogo.pdf

Between me and you—focusing on interpersonal relationships

Emotional regulation—focusing on self-direction and management

A Way Out—focusing on dealing with stress, danger, and crisis situations

Me and my identity—focusing on strengthening one's identity and sense of self

Self-management—focusing on managing oneself during learning, leisure, and work

The BEAMS program also includes the Educational Resilience program developed by the Harris Foundation for children at risk. The program is aimed at teaching children to handle everyday stressful situations. This, in turn, will provide them with psychological resilience and the ability to handle difficult situations.

The hottest topics in education in the past few years are **mindfulness and empathy**. In order for educators to teach these behaviors, they must first be able to use them themselves. They are required to learn and practice the skills in their own environment and toward their students. Thus, the teachers can "practice what they preach." The contemplative perception of education is the perception of teaching and education as focused on connecting the educator's inner life with their visible actions (Rogers & Raider-Roth, 2006).[10]

Kaniel (2013)[11] explains that "the meaning of empathy *is to feel and understand the personal world of the other as if it is our*

---

10 Rodgers, C. R., & Raider-Roth, M. B. (2006). Presence in teaching. *Teachers and Teaching: theory and practice, 12*(3), 265-287

11 Kaniel, (2013), **Empatia Bechinuch - chinuch beahahva [Empathy in Education - Education through love],** Hotzaat Machon Mofet

own, but without losing ourselves to the other. Meaning, a person experiences the thoughts, emotions, and behaviors of another person while maintaining full separation between himself and that person." In practice, we are talking about the ability to walk in the other person's shoes at any given moment, understanding their emotions, thoughts, and essence, whether they are positive, negative, or neutral, and provide judgment-free support without identifying with the other person completely. Kaniel (2013) adds that the basic values that can prompt empathetic actions justify the extreme mental effort needed to instill them. He points to three:

1. Acknowledging the value of the other out of fellowship with other humans
2. Acknowledging the importance of maximum inner freedom
3. Faith in the ability of all people to grow and change

The use of empathy enables a process that contains listening, mirroring, and an educated response, as well as addressing several layers of the discussion or situation from an emotional and logical perspective. It requires those involved, two or more, to give and receive.

Educational empathetic behaviors begin with a sincere interest from the first moment the student enters the educational system: How is the student, did they eat something that morning, what is their body language projecting, and so on. At younger ages, **a hug for a student that is willing to accept it** can always add. With students in elementary schools, you can add **marking or self-reporting on an emotions board** at the entrance to the school or the class, as this shows interest, and, with the older students, **an**

honest conversation. Some of us may have seen clips online where the educator receives each student as they come in and uses a shared sign with them. That's fine when it suits the educator, but there are plenty of other ways, as long as we truly see each student as they enter the school.

Several schools around the country have been wise enough, in my opinion, to go back to the old way of having the teacher wait in the classroom for the students, even if it means being fifteen minutes early. I worked with classrooms where we called this ritual **"Good morning, class."** The main purpose of this ritual, and ones like it, is to observe the students and listen to them at the start of the day. Did they come in, how did they arrive, how are they feeling, are they missing anything, and so on. The start of the day can have a significant effect on how the whole day goes. You can always combine this time with activities for relaxation or encouragement like a riddle, current affairs, presenting behavioral goals, and so on. It is better not to include management of behavioral issues during this time since it is not the time nor the way.

Thus, **emotional management, ventilation, and putting feelings into words** can be part of the regular class schedule. The means must match the needs and the expressive abilities of the students. The very legitimate declaration of how a student feels here and now, can often already suggest the replies and solutions to their problems, whether by discussing it with the student or by asking, directly, what they need right now, in congruence with what can be done in reality.

It can be done using:

An emotions board - in which each student has a representation using either their name or an image. Additionally, you have a pool of emotions for each student to choose from and put by their name. The emotion can be placed and changed once or multiple times a day. It can be a word, an image, an emoji, or a blank card.

Self-reporting - on a personal chart of emotions, similar to one of behavior, with a combined decision about the discourse about it.

Personal reflection notebook - with a choice when in the day, we write in the notebook.

A pantomime game - of presenting emotions and feelings using mimicry and body language.

Couple discussion: empowerment and giving - five minutes in which the students are divided into pairs. Each member of the pair shares their feelings and verbally empowers their partner or shares something that went well. The act of sharing also teaches that that sharing when confused helps to keep the importance of organized cognition in their consciousness all day long.

Giving permission to speak by throwing a sponge ball back and forth **or creating a tapestry by** passing a ball of yarn. The last activity strengthens the understanding that everyone has something going on but if they pass the yarn back and forth, a group tapestry will be created.

Every action that enables the students to take time to explore what they feel , will provide time to acknowledge experiences of success and empowerment, which will invite an aware verbalization of feelings and emotions, that consequently, will affect how they function for throughout the day.

Another program that can increase the students' motivation, after we've taught the subject and during the practicing of skills of mindfulness and empathy, is a weekly program to **reward students who practice inclusion.** This program is not necessarily about the inclusion of the other, but praising those who stood out in their behavior for promoting that goal in front of their fellow students. Just as we give excellence awards for social achievements and moral ones, we should empower those who contribute to the daily experience of emotional and social learning.

Finally, if we learn how to incorporate into the school curriculum elements of identifying and mirroring emotions and the appropriate reactions to them, then we allow our students to internalize and implement everything we wish they knew how to achieve. We could use one of the primary principles of bibliotherapy without crossing our boundaries as educators: **distancing to achieve closeness.** Of course, we must choose content that does not bring us into a therapeutic situation or, at the very least, assures our control of the discourse. In distancing to achieve closeness, we always discuss someone else. It's never us, never here. The intelligent transfer to ourselves happens when the student becomes an advisor to someone else. When we incorporate these actions in subjects like Literature, Tanakh, History, or any field with characters, situations, and plots, we make academic learning relevant to school life.

Examples for tools that connect to characters and can be adapted to different ages and needs:

1. Solving the characters' conflicts, problems, and dilemmas
2. Rewriting decisions or actions of the characters in preselected texts

3. Charting the behaviors, actions, emotions, and decisions of the characters
4. Using picture stories in an age-appropriate way
5. Guided film/clip watching exercises to identify emotions, situations, and reactions

Finally, if we know how to cancel out what we think is obvious about our students and their social and emotional functions, we can value them, direct them, give them feedback, and teach them. We can do all this at the same level of professionalism we use for our chosen disciplines and be loyal to ourselves and our students and provide the opportunities for mature, flexible, adjustable, and resilient education: an education that is wider than any single discipline.

CHAPTER 8

CLASSROOM LEARNING CENTERS: ADAPTIVE TEACHING AT ITS BEST

Have you ever seen the look in a student's eye when first seeing a learning center in class? There is always awe, curiosity, and a lot of appreciation ("What, you made all this for us?")

Meaningful learning relies on three main principles: providing value for the student and society; involvement of both the student and the educator; and relevance to the student.

Providing value for the students and society: awakening curiosity in the students, challenging the students and society, and contributing to both students and society.

Involvement of the student and the educator: learning should be active, experimental, experiential. It helps encourage a more profound understanding, more structuring of knowledge, and accepting responsibility by all those responsible for the learning situation. **Relevance:** learning is connected to knowledge and a curriculum. It is suited to the student's characteristics, interests, terminology, strengths, needs, and emotional functions in a changing world and a reality that requires constant adaptation.

The learning center is one of the most meaningful platforms for the implementation of meaningful adaptive education. A learning center is precisely what the name implies: a place where all the learning is centered around. It is a type of learning environment that helps develop the independent learner and is planned in such a way that it becomes the central scene of learning for the students for specific topics. It is a coherent element of the natural learning environment and is suited to the strengths and different needs of the students. Using the learning center, the student can take control of the learning process under the planning, supervision, and guidance of the educator. The use of it can, as mentioned, encourage independent learning in various modalities and methods, personal progress, pace, levels of thinking, and internal, external, or combined feedback and evaluation.

The educational platform that enables the learning center can be permanent or changing, in one unit or modular, and on the classroom walls or mobile. It also allows flexible movement between whole-class activities, small group activities, and individual ones.

It can serve various educational goals:

- **Instilling center** - a center through which we teach new topics
- **Accompanying center** - a center that takes a topic from the lessons and establishes, implements, and widens it. It also allows the students to study it.
- **Enrichment center** - for learning subjects outside the educational curriculum. Alternatively, to develop skills, strategies, life skills, different functions, and more.

- **Combination center** - one that combines the three centers above.

The size of the learning center can change based on plans and goals. Accordingly, the center can also be changing or permanent.

The organization of the structure and its pieces around a single organizing element is invaluable for creating organized thinking and systematic connections. For instance, the use of a story-based framework or that of a specific topic (examples to follow) helps define clear procedures and enables the students to identify with the learning center and connect it to their world. The dramatic effect of the framework story gives depth to the learning environment and provides challenges and support. It also serves as material around which the educator can frame their lessons and classroom behavior.

Returning to the good old ways?

Yes, sort of. When I was a student of education (it was a long time ago, but I will never forget it), we used to create the whole learning environment and its content with our own two hands, using synthetic materials, polypropylene sheets, cardboard, scissors, glue, etc.

However, we must understand that while the basic concept remains, times change, and we can now use other materials such as recycled and reused materials when possible, printed materials, or computers and applications like PowerPoint presentations, shared documents, and so on.

As long as the perceptual framework includes the advantages of using learning centers for adaptive teaching and is centered around the students, there is no creative limit, and one can upgrade the methods and tools to meet modern standards.

Hard work?

Yes, in the beginning. However, the more practiced one becomes planning and executing, the more natural, easy, and even fun it becomes. It becomes a way of life. Educators are no strangers to hard work, and teaching never promised to be a bed of roses, but that's not why we are here.

Does it require artistic talent?

No, it requires planning and creativity.

Does the educator have to work alone?

No. Students can help build the center. Small groups of students can be given specific tasks. Creating the learning center then becomes a means for adaptive evaluation for the students.

WORK STAGES:

- **Learning** - choosing a subject and learning about it as much as possible
- **Planning** - rationale, goals, creating topics, subtopics, and a framework story, adaptive activities, and methods of feedback and evaluation
- **Execution** - creating the center while taking into account time, materials, accessibility, design of the classroom, and class activities.

The Learning Stage—including data collection and mapping
We should ask ourselves:

1. What content has already been taught, and what is relevant today?
2. What are the predominant interests of the class?
3. What are the class's skills and educational and social preferences?
4. What needs, difficulties, and abilities stand out in class? They can be divided into levels or changing functions: perceptual, learning styles, skills, deciding on the main goal for the center.
5. Learning the chosen subject beyond the level of the learner, understanding its connections, and possible expansions for cognitive transference.
6. What resources do we have in order to properly learn the subject and later plan and implement it?

The planning stage

We will establish a rationale to use in the learning center. The usage should match the goals for the content and the functions of the learner (will be elaborated on later), the method of work, and the learner's characteristics, needs, and age. The rationale will refer both to the process and the results as well as their evaluation methods.

We will create goals—general and behavioral, operative, both in the content and the learner's functions.

We will map the subject into units, the number of classes, and subtopics.

We will develop a framework story that is relevant to the students or challenges them. This story will also provide the connections between the various sections of the center. It will internally motivate the students to advance and find out more using the educational microcosmos that we are creating.

We will plan a selection of adaptive activities according to the various relevant considerations for our students. Additionally, we should consider whether we prefer familiarity or innovation.

We will plan feedback and evaluation methods to follow the progress of the class, to allow the students to track their own progress, and to create internal and external feedback.

Examples for planning distribution

Credit: pedagogical teaching staff, 2nd class, special education, Seminar Hakibutzim College

Topic:

Lesson / Activity	Lesson 1 (45 minutes)		Lesson 2 (45 minutes)		Lesson 3 (45 minutes)	
	Adaptation A	Adaptation B	Adaptation A	Adaptation B	Adaptation A	Adaptation B
Activity 1						
Activity 2						

Topic:

Lesson / Activity	Lesson 1 (90 minutes)		Lesson 2 (90 minutes)		Lesson 3 (90 minutes)	
	Adaptation A	Adaptation B	Adaptation A	Adaptation B	Adaptation A	Adaptation B
Activity 1						
Activity 2						
Activity 3						
Activity 4						

	Mobile learning center	Wall based learning center
Design	Aesthetic, accessible, and adapted to the topic	
Size	Adapted to the content, students, and environment	

Lesson topic				
Operative goals for the content and the functions of the learner				
Activities and considerations for choosing them **Add all the relevant appendices	1		2	
Adaptations **Add all the relevant appendices	A	B	A	B
Feedback and evaluation (teacher \student)				

The example is taken from a poster that represents the process; credit: Danny Cohen

Used in 9the grade in a class with students who have complex learning disabilities, multifunctional learning disorders:

THE TOPIC OF THE LEARNING CENTER "AND THOU SHALT LOVE"—A JOURNEY TO THE HEART

Rationale

The students of the class that I teach, defined as the 9th grade for students with complex learning disabilities, often struggle to accept people who are different or to have empathy toward their friends who are going through complicated experiences. Additionally, many of the students suffer from low self-esteem as a side effect of their learning disabilities. And, depending on their age, there is a need for functional adequacy since they are soon starting high school. The idea of the learning center is that every student goes on a personal journey that becomes a class journey centered around acceptance, lack of judgment, compassion, and self-efficacy.

General goals for content

- Improving the ability to perform reflective processes concerning the learning process.
- Enriching the students' general knowledge about values and life skills
- Acquiring tools to deal with difficulties
- Experimenting with complex content that is not in the curriculum such as life skills, values, and compassionate communication skills

General goals concerning the learner's functions both personal and interpersonal

- Raising awareness of others' needs and accepting differences
- Improving self-efficacy
- Using the rules of conversation in class
- Acquiring compassionate communication skills
- Increasing listening and empathetic thinking skills

Education methods

The methods that served me were: teaching in front of the whole class, working with groups divided by level, independent work

Teaching tools

1. Worksheets adapted by level
2. Arts & crafts: drawing by assignment, creating sand bottles
3. Thinking games and emotional play
4. Interactive activities

Examples for demonstration aides

Pictures, cue cards, lightbulb moments, navigation and review, worksheets, workbooks, video clips, arts and crafts, models, games, products, and more (all can be used in either physical versions or digital applications).

Examples for control aides

Tracking charts, stickers, cards, transparency sheets for the worksheets, answer key, a final product that indicates the assignment's success, and so on.

EXECUTION STAGE

We will use all the means we have, creatively and enthusiastically, to implement the learning and planning stages. Then, we will implement the learning center in class or preschool and see it achieve a life of its own in a multilayered interaction with the students.

The center must be stable, accessible, aesthetic, visible, and user-friendly.

INCORPORATING THE LEARNER'S FUNCTIONS IN THE 21ST CENTURY:

The learning center today is a learning arena for students born into the 21st century. These are students who were born into the digital age and into many interests that are easily accessible to them. They know how to connect them to the relevant aspects of their life. The world has changed and, with it, the essences of the how, what, and why questions.

Therefore, the earlier we learn to map the needs of our students and match the content and goals to them, the more we have enhanced the educational value of their present and future.

Here is a distribution of the learner's functions in the 21st century as presented in 2014 by the Ministry of Education.[12] Educated use of this distribution means considering it during every stage of planning and implementation in a way that incorporates the functions together with the content and goals we have created for our students.

The learner's required functions in the 21st century	Valuable learning, teaching, and evaluation processes adapted for the 21st century (focusing on values, involvement, and relevance)	Results and achievements at the learner's level
Deeper understanding of the knowledge base as defined by the curriculum and elective subjects (cognitive)	☐ Development of different levels of thinking throughout the learning process ☐ Experiencing relevant implementation of the learned material and transference	☐ Meets the required achievements ☐ Implements the material learned in new situations in the same field ☐ Structures knowledge and insights and expresses them

---

12 The Ministry of Education (2014), Halomed, hamelamed, vema shebeinehem - metfisa leyisum [The Learner, the Teacher, and Between the Two - From perception to implementation]. https://meyda.education.gov.il/files/HighSchool/lomed_melamed_29052014.pdf

Critical thinking (cognitive)	☐ Learning to distinguish between opinions and facts ☐ Learning to determine the reliability of information sources ☐ Experiencing dilemmas that require **involvement**, moral judgement, and making a stand	☐ Asks questions ☐ Examines alternatives ☐ Makes fact-based decisions ☐ Presents a well-reasoned opinion
Creative thinking (cognitive)	☐ Learning to brainstorm ☐ Experiencing identifying and solving **relevant** problems for the learner ☐ Encouraging innovation ☐ Encouraging personal and group expression using various means ☐ Legitimizing expressing one's opinions, asking challenging questions, and learning from mistakes	☐ Comes up with original ideas ☐ Expresses divergent thinking ☐ Uses various methods to express themselves ☐ Creates innovative products from their studies
Reflective thinking (metacognitive)	☐ Incorporating reflective thinking processes as an integral part of executing tasks ☐ Experiencing analyzing mistakes, successes, and the **value** to the learner	☐ Uses reflection and adapts their products accordingly ☐ Improves learning products every time

Teamwork (interpersonal)	☐ Developing learning and task execution skills and activity in both the relevant real and virtual world while utilizing experiences and reflective processes	☐ Uses appropriate interpersonal communication ☐ Is willing to give in and is considerate ☐ Accepts authority and uses authority when appropriate ☐ Participates in tasks and contributes to the final group product
Respectful and productive conversations (interpersonal)	☐ Exercising conversation skills in the real and virtual world ☐ Encouraging situations in which conversation is vital to complete a task or process in which both parties are interested and find **relevant.**	☐ Uses conversation to create agreement, exchange opinions, and execute tasks according to needs ☐ Open to new ideas and opinions ☐ Acts ethically in the real and virtual spaces
Giving back to society, the family, the class, the school, the community, the state, and the general society **(interpersonal)**	☐ Encouraging and valuing initiatives that provide merit to society	☐ Takes part or initiates volunteer work, projects that have value to society

Accepting responsibility (interpersonal)	☐ Encouraging a variety of assignments and roles that the learner perceives as having **value** and using reflective processes after performing them.	☐ Is diligent performing their role ☐ Improves their performance ☐ Conducts themselves safely in the real and virtual worlds
Motivation (interpersonal)	☐ Encouraging learning according to varied and **relevant** interests to the learner and using their choice of learning methods ☐ Encouraging and valuing effort, success, initiative in the learning process	☐ Invests time and effort in learning even when it is difficult, high cost, or entails failure ☐ Initiates a deeper learning of the material
Self-efficacy (interpersonal)	☐ Experiencing **relevant** and adapted tasks for different learners ☐ Encouraging successes ☐ Encouraging challenging tasks ☐ Sharing evaluations for the sake of learning	☐ Believes in themselves and their abilities ☐ Strives continuously for success ☐ Handles new situations effectively ☐ Evaluates their own performances objectively ☐ Shares their emotions

Independent learning (management of learning)	☐ Choosing content, learning methods, learning partners, and so on. ☐ Developing skills in order to use information from various sources intelligently and represent that knowledge in various ways ☐ Exercising goal setting, planning how to achieve them, performing said plans, and evaluating the results using short-and-long-term tasks ☐ Developing digital technology skills	☐ Executes an independent learning process, including: ☐ Asks questions ☐ Defines goals ☐ Creates a working plan to achieve goals ☐ Executes the plan while: using various sources of information, evaluates them, using efficient methods to receive and distribute information ☐ Self evaluation of the process and final product ☐ Behaves ethically and safely in the real and virtual worlds
Sensory-motor learning (sensory-motor)	☐ Combining sensory-motor experiences into learning: spacial awareness, coordination, posture, aesthetics, music	☐ Represents learning using motion, sound, color, and shape

CONSIDERATIONS FOR USING TEACHING METHODS IN THE LEARNING CENTER:

Our work isn't over once the learning center enters the classroom. We provided the structure and the management. Now we need the fuel, the energy, for the educational explosion. Here is where we come in in a slightly different role than previously familiar. Now, we become guides, hosts, supervisors (occasionally), and, mostly, agents. In a class with a learning center, just like in any other, we are responsible for opening the lesson, for providing its main content, and for summarizing it.

In the ilnstilling center - we are responsible for providing access to the knowledge framework and skills during the start of the lesson as well as guiding the students' conduct during the main part of the lesson. If we choose to do this using frontal instruction, this does not mean we are keeping the teacher as a lecturer format. We can do this using many methods and means, such as investigating, to find out the topic, a game to connect the topics sections, creating definitions, conceptualization, exposure, presenting examples, guided exercises, and anything we can imagine. During the main part of the lesson, we will focus on studying in a manner suitable for our students. The summary will organize the information learned throughout; allow us to collect and revise terminology; and hint at the content of the next lesson: "where we go from here", which provides continuity and creates expectation. This is also the time we collect reflective information, as much as possible, from the students in order to mark for both them and ourselves the level of understanding and internalizing of the information that was achieved, how much of the goals we created has been accomplished, and the level of flexibility required from us in situations where not everything was achieved that we planned to achieve. If we know where we came from, we will know where we are headed.

In the accompanying, enrichment, and combination centers, we can use the same considerations but be flexible about the way we divide our time. For instance, we might want a shorter beginning, a longer and more varied main section, and the necessary summary.

Deciding on the method: It is all a question of goals. We should consider the goals for the content as well as for the students' functions. We can always navigate between several methods even while we aim for one goal. If we choose to focus on students' personal goals and differential advancement, we should allow more independent work. If we choose to focus on interpersonal functions, communication, altruistic behavior, and the social environment, we will provide more group tasks. Occasionally, we may want to combine personal empowerment with group contribution and cognitive functions and would consequently allow shared learning. Shared learning, as mentioned in previous chapters, will provide us with a process and results that are new, innovative, creative, and express companionship that is not necessarily based on friendship.

A quick important word on reflection:

As reflection is the best tool in education to create progress, it provides a roadmap for the student. You can use reflection in many ways: written, verbal, song, a play, personal, with the whole class, etc.. The role and importance of reflection are repeated throughout the book because it is a mediator for the students' internal dialogue and provides both a compass and anchor. The student gains self-efficacy and empowerment because they feel they have the control over the material learned, the method of learning, clearing the fog of material yet to be absorbed, and creating expectations for the future. This is known as "learning controlled consciousness."

Test yourself for a moment:

It is likely that everything you have read is already familiar to you, one way or another.

The organization, the conceptualization, and the highlights: did they themselves cause you to plan learning activities around the subjects you teach? Around topics? Around students that you know? Your class or kindergarten?

If you have suddenly connected more pieces of the puzzle, then you too are going through an adaptive process.

CHAPTER 9

ADAPTIVE DISTANCE LEARNING THROUGH THE KEYHOLE: WHO HOLDS THE KEY?

In the past year, we have all had to (and still have to) cope with the Covid-19 pandemic. The pandemic, along with other consequences, has emphasized the need for digital learning and the incorporation of learning technologies. It opened a window of opportunity to make learning more accessible in an online synchronous manner, or even not online and asynchronous. It also forced us to adapt learning to the characteristics of the modern student, the student of the digital age.

Alongside the opportunities, we face new challenges: navigating the class and managing behavior from afar, the need of the teacher to feel in control, the need to close the generation gap when it comes to technology, the need to create "something new, something else" that is suited to the new situation.

Learning from afar, synchronous or asynchronous, or classroom digitation that, lacking the teacher's constant control, can also be considered distance learning, requires adaptation of various executive functions to the changing reality, whether by choice or force. As the name suggests, it aims to teach.

Despite all the background noise of the distant but very real environment of the student at any given moment, or maybe because of it, the central part of the success of distance learning relies on advanced planning. Thus, the reward and profit of the involved parties will be precise, maximized, and empowering.

When we come to plan distance learning-teaching or learning with relative distance, we should ask ourselves several **focused questions** to formulate **precise goals**:

1. What is the **motivation** of the student to learn from afar? Until now, we, the teachers and parents, have accustomed the student to connect learning with the classroom and school, and with a teacher and a board.
2. What is the **need** which learning comes to fulfill? Is it acquiring content? Studying or rehearsing what has already been learned? Maintaining social connections? Measuring and tracking emotions? Fun time? Or something else?
3. What is the **scope** of learning, and what is its frequency? The length of time, the number of activities and terminology, the size of the study group, a class? A group? Alone? The number of skills required and the level of mental effort must all be predefined to clarify the situation for the student, parent, and teacher. We will aim to define the limits of learning based on the proverb "know where you are coming from and to where you are going" and reassure everyone by using a framework and a clear roadmap.
4. What is the **communication** pattern we wish to establish? Conversation with clear rules, a written answer, a chat, notes, or structured brainstorming using an online application, an email, emojis, peer presentations, the teacher as a host, presentations by the students, use of body language, sign language, pantomime, sending nonverbal visual products?
5. What will be the teaching-learning **modality**? Lectures, conversations, games, quizzes? Maybe a combination of several modalities? Do you have to sit in class? Can you stand? Move?

Is the lesson online, synchronous, recorded, or maybe not recorded, offline, asynchronous? Is the learned material documented in some way? Can you watch it again? Should we use WhatsApp groups? Incorporate voice clips, video clips, written reactions, and emojis?

6. What will be the end **product?** A process is also a type of product. Immediate? Postponed? Built-in stages that accumulate? Spiral or a combination of units? Solo? Group? Shared?

7. What aids do we supply in order to provide for the differences between learners? Strategies of perception, multi-perceptual teaching? Memorization strategies? Strategies for focusing? And all while taking into consideration processes of input, processing, and output.

8. **How do we evaluate?** Is it right to use the traditional methods? Is there an internal logic to test students from afar while limiting their access to the web or consulting with friends? Maybe it is not necessary? Possibly, the removal of old habits can create alternatives adapted to the new times and target audience?

9. What is the **feedback** we're expecting? Immediate - external or internal? Verbal or nonverbal? Rejected - written, handed in? Written reflective-verbal, metacognitive?

My educated colleagues who specialize in learning technology claim that, during ordinary times, in school, it is recommended we allocate 30% of the learning time to the incorporation of technological roles in teaching and learning. There is room for many additional functions that have become necessary to the development of the student, such as conversation and communication functions, social functions, emotional functions, behavioral functions, functions of initiative, and more. However, given the current challenges, we are forced to consider these functions and dedicate time to them.

Current terminology has taken root in our minds and forced us to reinvent or possibly renew old ideas and methods. Reality is forcing us to stay relevant, flexible, adaptable, cancel out the obvious, and move forward through uncertainty as we have little to no control over the future. However, we must still take responsibility for what we can control.

Only after we have dedicated time and thought to planning these elements, can we construct the classes.

We should present all the elements in every class, before, during, and after in order to allow the student and, depending on their age, their parents, to navigate the class easily. We can create an identification card for each class, for instance:

Element:	Goal/s:	Content and methods:
Motivation		
Need		
Scope		
Method of communication		
Modality/ies		
Product/s		
Aids and adaptations for differences among students		
Evaluation methods		
Feedback		

Examples for digital applications for moving a class into distance learning

Digital jigsaws, aimed mainly at junior high and high school students

If our goal is to progress in the material, we will divide it into units and create primary groups of students. Each group will receive the materials of one unit for study and investigation. Then, the groups will create a presentation and materials for explanation, illustration, and memorization.

We, the teachers, will then divide the class into secondary groups, groups with representatives of each of the units that include all the students. We will create a schedule for simultaneous presentations where each representative presents the materials that the primary group has prepared. The teacher will be present at each of these presentations, at least part of the time.

Each group can meet at a different time, but the end product must be shared. It is also acceptable to divide the students into online rooms. Then, the teacher can move between rooms, see what is going on, and provide guidance.

At the same time, we should create a shared Google Drive for all the groups, preferably in the form of a chart with categories of the topics and criteria for each unit. Thus, we have created a well-thought-out shared product of a vast subject with summaries created by the students under the teacher's guidance.

This method is also suited to project-based learning, research work, studying for tests, and so on.

Days will tell:

As a teacher of teachers and a fan of reflective processes, I asked my students to examine, in writing, the challenges and advantages of distance learning, mostly because they were required to utilize the applications of adapted learning (yes, I require, but I also get to see the final product).

Here are some things that came up from the recent and challenging experience both with classroom and individual teaching:

- In individual distance learning, it is possible to identify the personal adaptations each student needs; to precisely meet their needs; and to create interest, curiosity, and pleasure while adding images and videos that are connected to the child's interest and associating them to the learning goals as they were worded.
- Working with a computer allows many methods of teaching, from presentations; conversations; worksheets; study videos; special work pages; applications that help the student stay in contact with the teacher such as Wizer Me, Padlet, Mentimeter, and other applications that are connected through the school network such as educational websites or digital books and workbooks.
- The new reality of Covid-19 forced an intergenerational adaptation to technology, removed many blocks teachers had toward technology and computers, and even became an enriching experience of knowledge, education, and teaching that challenged, empowered, and increased self-efficacy.

- At the level of the learner, distance learning enabled flexibility with access to knowledge without regard to time and distance and enabled more personal adaptations for pace and level of learning.
- The offline asynchronous aspect allows for learning that is not dependent on a specific time so that every student will have the ability to watch the recorded lesson without the need to be physically present at any given moment. This forces the students to utilize time management functions, responsibility, and independence, and the feedback allows us to empower the student concerning these aspects.
- Every lesson is a house call. Especially when the student is learning from home, one can sense and get to know the environment in which they live, the level of comfort, or their hardships. Additionally, making the social system accessible in the student's house creates a feeling of belonging to the group and helps dissipate the feeling of loneliness many students feel, all under the guidance of a responsible adult.
- Additionally, during an online lesson, the teacher must play multiple roles and must activate, create connections, and awaken the students while maintaining control throughout the class and managing the participation of the students and their involvement.
- Many teachers have returned to work in teams. Groups have been opened to share advice, materials, and opinions, and not only between the staff of any given institution. There are no acceptance requirements: teachers, preschool teachers, guides, and any educational staff can

all contribute and benefit according to their needs. We are witnessing the return of sharing and altruism.

You can see that the focus of the insights mentioned is vast, and the list is still unfinished. We are now at the height of a process of change. Occasionally, time is required for matters to incubate and mature until we can draw conclusions and understand the implications of what changes will last and affect the generation, even after the storm has subsided.

Just like each student has strengths and weaknesses, so do teachers. The wide range of possibilities allows the teacher to prioritize adaptations for themselves and challenges them to learn and develop in order to enable adaptive learning for their students as well.

Only time will tell...

PART 2

INSPIRATIONAL STORIES OF ADAPTATION AND CHANGE

∽

*"Not everything that is faced can be changed,
but nothing can be changed until it is faced"*

(James Baldwin)

WHAT? HOW? WHY?

Throughout the years, I have met many inspirational people.

These encounters provoke discussions that often raise stories from a painful educational and developmental past. It is almost always possible to see the point in which everything changed: the point in which solutions emerged; ways of coping came up; perceptions of change and empowerment grew; and, mostly, people learned self-acceptance and went on to help others from their experience.

In this part, I have chosen to move aside and give center stage to five people who have agreed to reveal their personal stories, as much as they feel comfortable with at their current point in life. Because I felt the need to remain authentic, I have not made any changes to their choice of words or the length of the stories, elements that are influenced by age, their experience, and the intensity of the events in their lives.[13]

There is not enough time or space in a single book to include all the possible human relationships and outcomes that are born out of the encounter with hardship. In my view, even five stories can enlighten the reader about triggers, personal adaptive choices, and life-changing decisions that can shape one's reality and quality of life.

I have chosen, with love, to grant them the magic of giving.

---

13 Translator's note: the translation, of course, does not allow for this level of authenticity, I have tried to stay as true to the original style as possible.

Every one of the writers was willing to bestow their experience and expertise to others, to pass it onwards. For this reason, at the end of each story, I have added, with the writers' consent, their contact details. I invite you, the reader, to choose the "onwards" that suits you and to assist in promoting the methods implemented in this book and the stories.

Pleasant reading!

BREAKING GLASS CEILINGS

ZACH BEN SHMUEL

1. When things get tough, the tough get going

My name is Zach ben Shmuel, and I have made it my mission in life to make people smile. I am a husband to Galit, father of Maya, Noa, and Shira. I am a personal coach. I coach children and teenagers with Attention Deficit Hyperactive Disorder (ADHD), and I lecture and host groups and workshops. At the age of fifty, suddenly in the middle of my life, with a career and future as an officer in an elite military intelligence unit (in the IDF), life forced me to leave everything and to go on an unplanned journey. All of this, following a monumental event in my life. This discovery forced me to start a long, arduous, complicated, occasionally painful, and not simple at all, journey: my personal journey to life.

During this long journey, I discovered new things about my environment, my friends, and mostly myself and hidden strengths I never knew I had. I learned about perspective, what's more important, less important, and, mostly, I understood I needed to make a fundamental change to my life. I understood that life is too valuable a resource to waste on unimportant things and that I need to live in the here and now, to enjoy, accept, and cherish what exists.

In this chapter, I invite you to join me on a magical journey of self-discovery and change, from the belief that everyone has the right to take responsibility for their own life, experience success and happiness.

People say some childhood experiences are branded into the soul, that they shape us and turn us into what we are. For me, the experience has to do with stuttering.

As a child and a teenager, I had a stutter, a severe one. I always tell people that people thought I was mute until the age of five because I did not talk at all. Since then, however, I cannot seem to shut up.

Because of the stutter, I was also a very violent child. My main language, for a long time, was violence. I would hit everyone who made fun of me, or I thought was laughing at me, regardless of their age. Often, it was me who got beaten up, but it did not stop me from being violent since that was the only language I knew at the time, the only language that allowed me to protect myself and fight back.

Luckily, and it was good luck, the teachers I had in school knew how to accept me and guide me, and how to do a lot to get to know me. They were unwilling to cut me any slack, and, more than that, they were unwilling to give up on me. They were always there for me whenever I needed them, and there were many times when I needed them.

Additionally, my parents understood that something different should be done here. They regularly kept in contact with the teachers and management of the school where I learned and helped create one large support circle, a large and accepting circle that was made up of the system and my home—for me. This, I can confidently say today, helped me graduate after twelve years of school and was an important life lesson.

At the time, there was no junior high: elementary school lasted eight years, and in ninth grade, I moved directly to high school, where things were very different. I had to deal with a reality where nobody knew me, knew who I was, and, most importantly, did not know I stuttered.

At a certain point in high school, somewhere at the end of tenth grade, I decided, and I am not sure why, but I decided that I would make my stutter my best friend. This insight probably came from the understanding that my stutter and I were destined to be together forever and, if we were together, why not be friends? And so it was. I stopped seeing my stutter as a flaw and started looking at it as something that makes me unique. Everyone has something that makes them special. One person is too tall, one too short, one is fat, another is thin. And me? I stutter.

This understanding, especially its practice, demanded a lot of time out of me and a lot of effort, but the more I stuck with it, the less complicated my life became. Suddenly I could allow myself not only to play basketball but also to coach. Suddenly the stutter did not bother me, I could not only join the youth group Young Maccabi, but I could also join the counselors' course, finish it with honors, and become a counselor. More importantly, I could enjoy what I was doing, break glass ceilings and do what up until that point only seemed like a dream, never more than that.

Joining the army brought me again into a new framework. This time it was much larger, much more threatening, unfamiliar, and, mostly, a place where you got categorized from day one and carried that stereotype throughout your service. The selection process before the draft, and the service itself, meant I faced many glass ceilings in the form of attempts to dismiss me from officers' training and later from another course because of my stutter. These attempts and glass ceilings I broke in my unique successful way. This great success left me in the army for thirty-two years, twenty-two of which I served in an elite intelligence unit.

Today, when I look back on that long period, I can say that it was one great experience. A period that allowed me to shape who I am, build myself up, and turned me into what I am today. If I look at the period from the perspective of goal achievement, I have almost completely achieved all the goals I set for myself.

The ceilings I encountered have been almost all broken. The ceilings I could not break, I found creative ways around. I chose to look at this period from the point of view of the path. What can I learn from the amazing path I have traveled on since that day in July 1986 when I stood excited at the gates of the draft office until the beginning of January 2018? Then I went, together with my father, to a post-army trip to China, and that journey, which was long and not simple and demanded great strength of spirit, and forced me to face many difficulties, taught me some important things.

First, it taught me that **a smiling person can never be defeated!** And that no matter what happens with me in the future, I will always smile. Smiling is more than the chemicals it releases in the body. Smiling is a worldview, a belief, an understanding that in every bad thing there is also something good, a light that makes us see things differently and puts things in perspective. Smiling reminds us to take care of ourselves: of our physical and, maybe, more importantly, our mental health.

This curved path also taught me that life often brings surprises when we least expect them, and that it is good that it is that way, since if we expected them, we would be paralyzed and unable to do anything. Moreover, it is very important to enjoy what we have, the here and now. To get the maximum out of the current situation and stop claiming that life is unfair, or I did not get what I deserve.

Like my grandmother, God rest her soul, taught me, "The person who claims they didn't get what they deserved doesn't know how lucky he is."

2. Surprise? Victory!

Nothing I had been through could have prepared me for the greatest surprise of my life, a surprise that life brought me in 2015.

It was the fourteenth of January 2015, a Sunday, and it was pouring rain outside. I was halfway out the door of my military career, with an army pension, a new workplace, and plans for my second part of life almost all set up. I woke up to another ordinary long workday.

The thought of going out into the rain didn't thrill me, but I pulled myself together and got ready to leave. A moment before leaving, after I shaved, I felt something in my throat. From my perspective, I thought it was a growing infection, and I decided to go through the office, stop at the unit's doctor, and ask her for antibiotics. This is how I started the day that would turn my life upside down, a day that ended with me opening the website for the Israel Cancer Association and discovering that I have all four criteria for lymph node cancer.

It would take another two months from that day, four biopsies, and more testing until I got the confirmation for what I understood and knew much sooner: my life was going to turn upside down! The beginning was very hard. First, the time it took me to come to terms with this news and then to tell my immediate environment: my wife, daughters, parents, and family. I needed to take care of everyone, make sure they were all ok, and that they came to terms with the news and could move forward.

And, of course, one small thing: I needed to fight the cancer.

The first thing I did was determine the therapeutic process, which included chemotherapy and radiation, like a military operation. Why an operation? Because I was taught that a military operation is a short-term process, usually with a limited schedule, with a beginning, middle, and end. And this was how I decided I was going to view my therapeutic process.

Another insight was to find something positive in everything I had to go through. Every difficulty, every pain, every round of chemo or radiation. Despite the pain, the discomfort, the painful effects on the body and the spirit, I tried and often succeeded in finding a small light, a little firefly that turned the darkness into something else.

In the end, I decided, as much as I was able to, I would manage this operation, this disease, and not let it manage me. I would not let the negative feelings, the fear, and the uncertainty, take me over. I did this by telling myself that, true, I had cancer, but that **wasn't all I had, only one thing of many**. I had a lot of other positive things: I had a wonderful wife, three amazing daughters, two superb parents, two wonderful siblings, and many other positive things that gave me the strength to continue and, more importantly, put things in perspective.

What can't be simple, simply won't be

After I understood that I could not continue my life at the crazy pace I was used to, objectively it was too hard, I realized I needed to make a change. From the start, it was clear to me that I was not going to reinvent the wheel. My long journey as a commissioned officer and my service of twenty-two years in the intelligence core filled my life with insights, abilities, and many things that I would not lose or say goodbye to. The opposite was true: I was going to use them because this was the baggage I was coming with. This baggage, which had grown throughout my life and held all I had become, was an invaluable possession that characterized and defined me, made me who I am, and I was not going to give it up.

So what was I going to do? I understood that I had to find things that were unique to me, things I felt I was a world champion at and that, no matter what I did, would always be there for me. They would help me find myself and, with them, I would go on a journey to find myself. I decided that I was going to take my funnel of opportunities and open it upside down.

You're probably asking yourself, what is a funnel of opportunities? That is a very good question that I asked more than once until I understood this simple idea and the great advantage you get from opening it upside down.

Imagine a funnel into which you put, at the wider end, many things, including: what do you want to be when you grow up? What have you learned? What are the expectations of your parents, or your spouse from you? What are your dreams? What do you love? And many other things. After you've put everything into the funnel, you mix them up, push, and from the other side a type of dough comes out. Out come one or two things that are made up of all the things you put inside, that if you think about it are the things that characterize and make up what you are.

To open the funnel upside down means to go from the bottom to the top, from understanding and characterizing myself to what I can do with it.

What do you do? You find two or three things which you are really great at, those things that, no matter what you do or where you are, will always make you feel like you're on solid ground, and you go on a journey of self-discovery with them.

You're probably thinking, what does he want from us? It is prideful to say what I'm good at, and people will look at me strangely. My answer is that you don't owe anybody anything. You define for yourself, and only for yourself, what you think you're excellent at. These things, my friends, are your basic characteristics.

After you've defined these things for yourself, you go and search: what matches the characteristics you've defined? In my case, I decided I was a world champion at creating intimate interpersonal relationships and, secondly, that I could make people create meaningful changes in their lives.

With these two insights about myself, I went on a journey of discovery where I ended up finding, with the help of my amazing wife, that what I wanted to be was a personal coach. Once I understood this, everything else clicked into place, and, from there, the journey to a coaching course was very short. Once I finished it, I immediately started coaching. At the same time, I studied coaching for children and teenagers with ADHD, and finally, group coaching.

I beat cancer and grew into the next chapter

3. The small man in the radio receiver

As a small child, I found myself often taking apart radio receivers to find the small man hidden inside. I did not understand how people who hosted radio shows got inside the radio. I wanted to meet them, to see them, and to ask them many questions. I would dream that I, like them, went inside the radio and would talk exactly like Raya Admoni, Nili Hemeiri, and Motti Barkan who hosted the show Labat Velaben Velemi Shemitanyen[14] that was on the air every day at 1 pm on the radio channel Reshet Aleph, a show I would listen to regularly as a young boy.

The tens of radios transmitters I took apart during my childhood are proof I never found the small man in the receiver, but it is also proof that I was a curious boy with a creative streak since I had to put those machines back together again.

Later, when I studied for my BA in university, I worked as a security officer at the radio studios on Heleni Hamalka street in Jerusalem. One day, I heard a familiar voice at the gates. It was Raya Admoni, my childhood hero. I walked up to her, introduced myself, and excitedly told her the story about taking apart the radio receivers, how I searched for her for years and couldn't find her. I was very excited, and I felt that my childhood dream had come true. In this way, I found myself spending hours during my shifts in the radio studios and fantasizing about how I would one day host a radio show of my own.

"Seek and ye shall find"

Twenty years later, with that same dream, I became a guest on a radio show of a friend, a host of a show on the First Social Radio website. At the end of the show, my friend asked me, "How was it?" I answered with questions of my own "How can I host a show? Who do I need to talk to?"

I took the station manager's number from him, contacted him, introduced myself, and asked, "What needs to happen so I can make my dream of hosting a radio show come true?" I told him about my dream, about all the radio receivers I took apart, and about my search for the small man in the receiver. The station

---

14   Literally: For the girls and the boys, and whoever is interested

manager told me that all I had to do was really want it and that, if I did, I was welcome to come to host a show.

Since that conversation, I have hosted my own show on the First Social Radio called The Seventh Night - Nighttime Tales. The show is about people who went through a crisis and difficulties and used them to find the opportunity to make a change in their lives. Once every two weeks, I host a guest in the studio, and together we discuss their journey of change.

As for me? Every time I get to the station and go into the studio, I'm still hoping to find the small man in the receiver and tell him that dreams are made to be achieved and that I have achieved mine.

4. So, Mrs. Perspective, what have we learned?

I have learned that life is too valuable to waste on nonsense, and I should do everything I can, and maybe even more, to enjoy it. The underlying assumption of that point is that we are all going to die sooner or later, and if we agree on that, I have to ask you, where are we running to in this crazy rat race of life? To gain more stuff? Bigger things? Newer things? What does that give us?

I could not help remembering my grandmother's Alisa's saying, "Always remember that the queen of England and the poorest beggar in Leicester Square both eat with one fork and one knife, be it tin or gold, it doesn't matter. What matters is you can't eat with more than one knife and one fork."

If we looked at this race a little bit differently, we would see that we are running toward our end. So, I suggest we replace this race with a journey. We decide that, from this day onwards, we are going on a journey: a journey toward life, a journey in which we can enjoy the here and now, what there is and not what there is not. Enjoy the beauty of the world, and it is beautiful, believe me. With all the bad things it contains, the world is a beautiful place, and everything depends on the perspective we choose to have.

Once I realized this, I stopped running and began to walk. I left the crazy race toward nothingness and started my journey toward life. During this journey, I discovered amazing things that had already existed around me, but I was unable to see them because I had been in too much of a rush. Small, amazing things that fill the spirit with happiness: real happiness and not the fake kind. More importantly, I began to enjoy life, to value it. The more I looked around, the more I discovered things that made me understand that I was choosing the right path, marching confidently along my path in the journey of my life.

What else did I discover on this journey of life?

I discovered that the **world is full of good people** that are there to help you, to give you a hand, and to assist with no expectation of a reward. All I needed to do was to be ready to accept the help, to reach out my hand. The beginning wasn't easy at all. I had a difficult time admitting I needed help, that I, the all-powerful, needed someone to give me a helping hand and help me take a step forward.

Once I understood that my stubbornness not to allow people to help me, not to accept their assistance, was getting me nowhere fast, once I understood that those people will be there whether I accept their help or not, once I understood that I could profit greatly from that help, once I understood all these things, and agreed to accept them, my life changed and became more comfortable. The feeling that someone is willing to help me grew and spread and became part of who I am.

This discovery strengthened the insight that has become my mantra: **giving is receiving.** Giving, not to get material rewards of any sort, is to give from the very understanding that giving is a great honor. Since I have received this honor, I use it daily with every step I take.

Whether it be volunteering in different places, helping and accompanying people in extreme situations, or anything I am required to do, the rule I follow is that giving, like small things, should always be done with great love. And I give with a lot of love.

I also learned that **perspective is not a dirty word** and that one can and should use it and see the world in general and our difficulties in particular, with some perspective, since it makes life truer and better. It helps us understand that the world is not black and white and that the color palette is full of many colors and shades, and that using them makes our hardship more acceptable, definable, and manageable.

I understood that **crises are part of everyone's life,** and we should put them in perspective. That crises are things that can and should be managed, and that, more than anything, they can provide an amazing opportunity for a life change. I succeeded, and there is no reason you cannot. It all depends on your faith in yourself, in your own abilities and strengths.

Finally, in between all my work today, I remind myself every morning that I am waking up because life is too beautiful to waste on nonsense, that we need to listen to our hearts and follow them and smile and love a lot. I remind myself not to let fear take over my life, out of the understanding and faith that fear is the most contagious thing there is, but I can resist it because in my subconscious exists an insatiable desire for life.

Zach Ben Shmuel is a serial break of glass ceilings

Zach is a personal coach for adults, a coach for children and teenagers with ADHD, a lecturer, and a host of small groups and workshops. He collected all those insights, added them to his rich life experience and his expertise at motivating people to make meaningful changes in their lives, added tools from the personal coaching world and the positive psychology world, and wrapped them all with a lot of love and passion which he brings to life and to his lectures and workshops.

Among his lectures are **My Elephant and Me, The Freedom to Stutter, The Different is Equal**. These lectures and others are based on his extraordinary life story and the many insights he has achieved.

He also volunteers a lot, including in the children's unit in Dana Hospital in Tel Aviv, various nonprofits, accompanying cancer patients, and more.

To request lectures, contact him at benshmuelz@gmail.com

MY SELF-ESTEEM JUST DIVED OFF OF THE TALLEST BUILDING IN TOWN, OR DID IT?

SHANI SHUKRANI-TZARFATI

My story with adaptive learning begins with me, as a student, who would read her homework or tasks from empty notebooks already in elementary school. A child who spent half her time outside of classes in junior high until I reached the tenth grade. There was one teacher who noticed that I was always on the move and that I had trouble focusing (until today, by the way, I find it much easier to focus when I am moving than in any other situation). My teachers were frustrated by this, and one of the words I heard most often as a child was "bubbly." I never understood who that person was who decided that was a legitimate description of an ordinary person.

The first time I was diagnosed, I was sixteen. My mother, who wasn't used to getting calls because of me, was surprised to get a phone call from the history teacher who said that in her opinion, "it's worth getting her diagnosed." I was only sixteen and a bit in shock, and I didn't understand what that meant. Mom agreed, took out what was then a month's salary, and off I went to get diagnosed. The diagnosis felt like a cruel experience to me. I felt I was simply not good enough, a feeling I still have today every time I have to deal with an educational field or when I think about studying... not good enough!

When the diagnostician finished her diagnosis, she called my mother and me into the office and announced clearly, "Shani has a low IQ, dyslexia, dysgraphia, and ADHD. I suggest going to see a neurologist ASAP and getting her prescriptions for medications." There was a silence, and then my eyes began to tear up, tears that made it clear that my self-esteem had taken a dive off the tallest building in town. Mom laughed, I mean rolled over laughing and couldn't stop, to the point where she was crying from laughing. She took the form, and we walked away. At the bus stop, she looked into my eyes and said, "so one dumb diagnostician said that you're not smart. So she said it. You're a wonderful girl who will grow up to become a wonderful woman." At that moment, full of tears in my eyes, I no longer felt alone. My mother was and still is the first person on earth who ever believed in me, and I will always be grateful to her.

The next day, I sat down in the public library, took the findings of my diagnosis, and began to read up on learning disabilities, attention deficit hyperactive disorders, and everything in between. I discovered a million theories: I was "a rainbow child sent to the world to be fixed"; "There was no such thing as attention deficit hyperactive disorders"; "everything was my mom's fault for getting divorced, and this was a punishment from God." In any case, I had never seen a subject that caused people to speculate quite so much. In the end, I found a definition of dyslexia: "primary disability in reading, and sometimes writing." Then I continued to dysgraphia: "primary disability in writing." And then, I sat down to read about ADHD. I sat and read, and I learned everything there was on the subject that could be found. And then, I cried. I cried so much, I could not understand "why me" and how to cope.

My school counselor was a sweet woman but knew very little. My homeroom teacher also knew very little, but she covered it up with a lot of yelling, and, again, I felt alone. And then something happened, possibly some survival instinct kicked in. I searched on the internet "How do you learn with learning disabilities?" I went back to the library, I read a book on learning strategies, and I decided I was going to pass my *Bagrut tests!*[15] Even if no one would help me, even if the teachers could not understand, even if I had to sweat blood and tears to get my adaptations (known then as facilitations), I was going to pass my *Bagrut tests.* I learned a lot of new strategies, new ways of summarizing large amounts of material, and I found my most meaningful strength: I remember the material best when I am teaching it to someone else. So I began to teach anyone who wanted, anyone who agreed, and suddenly I had friends in class, because they needed me and knew me, and I was no longer invisible. Suddenly, teaching was my way to survive high school and it worked. I would sketch graphs and draw wars and summarize everything in three parts.

I finished high school with an average above 90 and a mother who told me at the end of twelfth grade "I knew you would succeed." I served in the army (IDF), and after the army, I decided I would do the psychometric exam.[16] I also decided there was no chance in the world that I would be a teacher, that it was a horrible profession, undervalued, and only depressed women worked in that field.

First, obviously, teachers are depressed since they work in the most obtuse system in the world. Secondly, they are obviously undervalued since no one takes them seriously, neither the

---

15 Israeli matriculation tests on different subjects, required to graduate.

16 In Israel, the psychometric exam, an exam similar to the SATs, is necessary to get into university (and different fields have different grade requirements). It is usually taken after high school and often after mandatory military service.

management nor the parents. Thirdly, it is a very lonely profession. That is to say, you are the one standing in front of the management and supervisors when something goes wrong, you are the one that has to face the parents, and you are the one facing the students. You are constantly exposed to criticism from every direction. By the way, when you succeed in your task, everyone gets the credit, everyone but you, the teacher.

Spoiler alert: as you can probably read between the lines, I went and got a degree in special education with a specialty in Tanakh, because a religious background can sometimes make life easier. The psychometric test was also a war of survival for me. Receiving adaptations for the psychometric is as easy as getting a negative tax return, seeing snow in Tel Aviv, or catching a unicorn. One of the craziest requirements was to bring a letter from an elementary school teacher describing my difficulties. I stared at that requirement: I was a girl who had just finished her military service. I had no idea where these crazy requirements came from. Why would a teacher remember me from eight years ago, and why would she agree to write such a letter? In the end, after appealing the requirements and going to an all-out war with the National Institute for Testing and Evaluation, I finally got my adaptations for the psychometric test. I think this experience made it clear to me that, even as an adult, having learning disabilities and ADHD means the war never ends. There is no institution in the country that is happy to give people the adaptations they require. Then I understood that I still had no idea what I wanted to be when I grew up or, in other words, what I wanted to study. My grade on the test was higher than the national average but still low for the fields I was interested in. I wanted a profession that helped people and made them better.

One of the days, by accident, I met someone I went to high school with. Together we had studied for the Bagrut test in history. He called out to me in the street from the other sidewalk, "Shukrani, stop for a second." I turned to him, and he said, "thank you" and smiled from ear to ear. I asked, "what for?" and he answered, "you remember that method you taught me to help me remember things?" I answered, "well, what about it?" and he said, "Well, I used it in the Non-Commissioned Officers' course, and I finished first in my class, thank you." And then he went on his way, and I was left standing there. At that moment, I understood I was probably going into the education field. The degree in special education was also complicated and challenging when it came to disabilities and adaptations. It included a lecturer in my first year who told me "There's no such thing as a teacher with learning disabilities," and the requirements for the Hebrew grammar course where I needed to learn *nikud* [symbols that serve as vowel markers in Hebrew and are rarely used in daily life], something that is pretty much impossible for someone with my disabilities. Throughout the degree, I often heard disparaging remarks from both students and lecturers. I had a feeling that no one really knew how to behave once you went past the slogans. I studied my first degree in a place that claimed to accept and include all the teachers it educated or, as they liked to call us, "teachers blossoms." I felt less like a blossom and more like a cactus or a weed, an outsider with disabilities that even the system could not handle.

In every course, I had to explain again to the lecturer. Some lecturers were insulted that I could not sit for an hour and a half, some lecturers responded to me explaining that I had difficulties writing with "So how are you going to be able to be a teacher?" As if I was a three-eyed alien. In any case, it was an experience that taught me that there are two messages: one said out loud, "we are all different and equal," and the other said silently, "you're a broken teacher."

The final confirmation came during my third year. Everyone I asked if I should tell the supervisor that I had learning disabilities told me, straight out, "no, let them get to know you, and then they can find out." The message was again and again, "hush! No one can know you have learning disabilities." The feeling was that I was being blamed for my disabilities. And then, I went to do my internship for the Ministry of Education. The Ministry of Education is, in my opinion, the most obtuse body imaginable. Someone who hasn't worked there cannot imagine the amount of bureaucracy, strange rules, notices, bizarre decisions, and a lot more. My year of internship as a homeroom teacher made it clear to me how much the system had not changed at all during the ten years I'd been out of it. I was accepted as a homeroom teacher in a class with behavioral difficulties in an ordinary school. My disappointment from the bodies who made and executed the decisions was extreme. There was zero acceptance, zero tolerance, zero acknowledgment of people, nothing like what I had learned and studied. But my students, my seven wonderful children, were worth the difficult year I spent there. At the end of the year, the principal made it clear to me that I would never be a teacher and an educator, and she refused to grant me my credits.

I, who was already used to the idea that the Ministry of Education and I were a failed love story, chose to appeal her decision. My appeal was accepted by the Ministry of Education, and I won. Today, however, I don't work for the Ministry of Education. I mostly fight against it.

Adaptive teaching was and still is my life jacket. It is the way I see the world. It is the source of my income, my help to my beloved students, and to myself. When I teach my students to create a to-do list for the next two weeks so that they can handle the workload, I do the same myself. I don't teach strategies that I don't fully believe in. I believe in adaptive teaching with all my heart. The idea that every student needs teaching that is personally adapted to them and their personal complexities is so logical and simple.

Adaptive teaching requires the person who does it to be creative, be innovative, listen, show an interest, and always be on the ball and learning. Adaptive teaching reminds every teacher that they were once a student, and keeps them constantly learning, constantly developing.

My students always ask me why I choose this specific profession. I think, if I had a teacher who taught me how to learn and what is right for me, my life would have been much easier.

I am Shani Shukrani-Tzarfati, twenty-seven years old, married to one man and a mother to one child, a teacher of adaptive teaching with a small business who believes anyone can succeed if only they had the right tools. It's all a matter of faith in the child and devoting time and energy to them because they deserve it![17]

Contact information: shukranishani@gmail.com

---

17   Shani is also currently studying for her M.Ed. in special education

I CAN CHANGE MY "TINY SQUARE"

CHEN KAKOV

My name is Chen Kakov. I am twenty-eight years old and have a B.Ed. in special education.

As a student, I had a challenging learning experience. I did not have an easy time at school: I was a very anxious student and did not like the way teachers used to teach. The teachers would mostly dictate the material.

I cannot remember a teacher that tried to stimulate my thinking as a student, except for very few. One of them was my ninth-grade homeroom teacher Mrs. LB, a wonderful woman who took me on as a project and helped me progress in my studies. A teacher who believed in me and told me I would get far because of my determination. LB knew that, at the same time, I was being bullied in school and that money at home was tight. She saw how hard I tried to focus and work hard in school and that I just "was not there" because my head was too busy thinking about the fact that I had no friends and that my home was falling apart. She took me aside to a conversation where I promised to "get a handle on myself" and do better. LB knew that the financial situation did not allow me to take a private tutor. She suggested I come to her house twice a week and she would help me in school, as long as I came with ready questions. For a whole year, she taught me to answer essay questions, manage math problems more easily, and believe in myself and my abilities. My achievements improved incredibly, and I became one of the top students in class.

After I finished my special education degree and teaching degree, my goal as a teacher was to mend the learning experience I had as a student and be like LB. I made a commitment to myself that, when I became a homeroom teacher, I would teach differently from how teachers in school taught me. I would be there for my students in difficult moments like LB was there for me, and like she saved me when I thought everything was falling to pieces.

During the first year as a teacher, I taught a class (with two grades 5-6) in a school for behavioral disorders. During the second year, I taught special education to students with complex learning disabilities in a regular junior high.

The reality of being a teacher in the Ministry of Education shattered my dream a bit. Despite all my goodwill and motivation, I often felt that I did not have enough tools to develop my students in the way I feel is best for them. I watch my students studying, as each one of them, one after the other, shakes their head and utter sounds of despair. This happens even though I have created experiential activities, added adapter worksheets, and combined technology with studying.

Their feeling of despair became my feeling of frustration, and after a while I became disappointed and even a bit repulsed by the system of education and teaching. Despite my despair, I did not give up and promised myself I would be there for my students. No matter what happened, I would do everything to help them succeed and believe in themselves as one of my teachers believed in me when I was a teenager.

The change in my understanding began when I had no other choice. I understood I could not change the entire education system, but I could change my "tiny square" in my class, as much as possible. So it was that despite the frustration, and out of listening to the needs of the students, I incorporated more technology in classes, more games, films, personal talks, like the students asked for and directed me.

Today, my confidence has improved. I know what I can do for my students. I know that no matter what I am told to teach, I will teach it the best I can and do everything so that the learning will be full of experience, will be successful, educational, interesting, and develop their thinking.

My message is that there is no limit to the abilities of a person, and if you really want something, you can achieve it with determination, willpower, and grit. I learned, and am still learning, that one should never give up, and even when things seem impossible, there's always a solution.[18]

---

18   These days Chen is studying for her M.Ed. studies in learning assisted technology

TURNING POINT–BECOMING A LEARNING-DISABLED EDUCATOR

ITAY BEN YAKAR

I will start with the perception of what a teacher-educator is for most people.

Many people ask me, "Why did you choose this profession? Don't you know you can't make money at it, that there is nowhere to advance?"

My answer is, usually, "This is the thing I love to do; I enjoy doing it, and if you do what you love and enjoy doing it, you don't need more than that."

But the honest answer is much longer and is connected to the name of this chapter: becoming an educator. Long before I even thought of becoming a teacher, I was that, and my best teachers were the ones that influenced me the most. I will try to explain how the boy became an educator and made his dream come true.

It all started when my parents registered me as a first-grade student in Kibbutz Shfayim. I was not from the kibbutz; I was an outsider, and I was seen as such. I did not belong. It was the same in the second, third, and fourth grades. From a child who loved and enjoyed life, I turned into a closed-up shy child, one that did not talk much.

My parents did not notice this, mostly because I didn't draw their attention to it. My father worked from morning until night-time. My mother would sometimes ask, "How was school?" I would answer that it was fine.

If I came home bleeding from school, from being beaten up, I would tell them I was playing soccer, and I had fallen, or things like that, and that was the end of it. Until one day in fourth grade, I couldn't take it anymore, and I fell apart.

I told my parents everything, everything I went through from the minute I got to school, the difficulties, and how the teachers ignored it. Yes, those teachers that were supposed to be present and notice such things. Right away, they took me out of school and searched for another school for the following year. During that time, I was mostly at home, alone with myself.

Even then I would think, how is it possible that kids behave like this? How is it possible that teachers don't look out for kids that need help, that are being abused? And I didn't find an answer, not yet...

After getting some advice and thinking it would be easier for me to catch up, I was transferred to a special education school in Tel Aviv: Masada school. I still remember the name of the street it was on, the names of the students who studied there, the name of the principal, and the names of many of the teachers. Oh, how I needed that school.

I had to fill in gaps in my education because most of it, up until that point, was determined by daily survival rather than learning. So, I stayed another year in the fourth grade. I managed to catch up pretty quickly but, more importantly, to meet other students who didn't look at me funny, and even liked me, so that I became one of the popular kids in class.

I remember there was an assistant there named S[19], who taught me as much as my homeroom teacher did. She taught me to play the card game Rummy and helped me with math, something I still have difficulty with today.

I was sent to be diagnosed only after I started at Masada school. The results showed that I had learning disabilities, that I had ADHD, and trouble writing.[20] Likewise, it was clear I had trouble in math, but I did not have Dyscalculia. This didn't bother me, of course, because I had friends and was getting an education. For the first time.

I finished fourth and fifth grade at Masada. My teachers and parents understood that I was too advanced for the school, and they needed to find a place that was more suited to my skills. I remember being afraid. Until I had found a place that accepted me, now I had to move to a new place? I did not say that to my parents. I knew they wanted what was best for me and that I would always have the opportunity to come back if worse came to worst.

I skipped the sixth grade and started seventh grade in Shafririm high school in Kibbutz Givat Haim (Ihud). So, that is a private school that belongs to the legendary Binyamin Shafrir who, after a brief introduction, decided I was suited to learn there.

There too, I met friends and learned according to my skills. My teacher in the seventh and eighth grades asked my parents why I was learning there and added, "He's very smart, the learning here

---

19 The names of the people in the story are shortened to their first initial, in order to protect their anonymity.

20 The professional terminology has not been updated to 2013 (DSM V) in order to keep the story authentic. Here: learning disabilities: specific learning disorders in reading, writing, math, and more. ADHD – attention deficit hyperactive disorders, with type and degree are usually presented.

isn't for his level, he should go to a regular school." My mother told her, "Here is where he belongs, he's happy here, and here he will stay."

In Friedrich Nietzsche's philosophy, he wrote that to become a "superman", to rise above your own maximum potential, you must first find a character to admire and imitate, someone you wish to learn from. I found this character in the eighth grade.

Teacher L, a teacher for science and chemistry, two fields I knew nothing about, was my first character on the way to being a "superman". He ran chemistry experiments with us, taught us about science and nature, explained astronomy, and I found myself fascinated in every lesson.

L saw in me then what I see in **myself** today: an educator in the making. He identified the interest I found in that subject and my desire to learn and teach it. I would teach my parents and my friends and tell him about it. He decided that I needed to help him pass on the information to other students, and so it was.

I would help him and teach the students who were a year or two years younger than me. I did that and felt amazing. I felt that this was a destiny I was creating for myself. I was in ninth grade, and I was making my own future.

In the eleventh grade, Bagrut tests started. I remember that I realized then that I needed to "overcome" my learning disabilities. At that point, I wasn't taking Ritalin. I objected to it. I tried by myself, and you can say I succeeded well.

I learned math at the math center of the school. Two teachers taught there. One of them, Y, who was one of the most amazing teachers I ever got to meet, helped me and even made me love the subject. I wasn't good at it, I didn't grasp it well, but I loved coming and learning, advancing, and switching topics. I managed to do one Bagrut unit,[21] and, for me, that was a success. I think it was because of Y, even though she would say it's because of me.

Aside from math and science, I also learned physics and drawing from an amazing teacher named LV, who was also the vice-principal.

LV was everything I think a teacher should be, an academic standup. He taught us physics, drawing, prepared us for our driving theory test, and made us laugh in each and every class. We enjoyed his lessons, and it never occurred to us to interrupt him because why would you interrupt a teacher whose classes you enjoy?

In twelfth grade, I began to worry about what was to come: the army, then life. None of us, the students, had yet to experience that. I will never forget that day. In the morning, I went to L, who was not my homeroom teacher but that of a different class in my grade, and I asked him, "L, how are we, students of special education, going to succeed in life? Who will employ us afterward? Won't we always be seen as incapable and incompetent?"

L looked at me for several seconds and didn't say a thing. Then he answered, "Itai, please collect all the students of the grade, tell them to come to the big class, never mind which class they're supposed to be in, please bring them, and go there." I did what he asked.

We sat down all of us in class and did not know what was about to happen. L, the teacher, began to talk, and this is what he said.

"I understand you have worries about what is about to come. You are facing a challenge that you still don't know how to deal with. One of the students was brave enough to ask me what is going to happen afterward, in life, at work, in the army, how will people look at you when they realize you have learning disabilities?

---

21 Translator's note: the standard range is between 3 and 5.

Well, I want to tell you something that I haven't been brave enough to say until today: I am learning disabled. I, who teaches chemistry, science, history for matriculation, civil studies, and am a homeroom teacher, yes, I am learning disabled. I have dysgraphia, which is why I never write but give you ready-made summaries. I also have trouble reading, which is why I ask you to read in classes. My dear beloved students, if you want to achieve something, you can achieve it, regardless of what stands in your way. You have to believe in yourselves and be afraid of nothing. Today I am not afraid, and it's because of you!"

Turning point. I didn't realize, then, the weight of that phrase. Everyone was silent. We were shocked. How was it possible that our most admired teacher, the smart one, the all-knowing, the one who teaches so many subjects, including subjects for Bagrut tests, how could he be learning disabled?

I looked at him admiringly, and I knew. He was the type of person I wanted to be like. He was the person I would model myself after. I wanted to be a teacher, I wanted to make my students believe what L just made me and everyone believe. **The teacher educator.**

I won't bore you with my time in the army, but my desire to become a teacher only grew. After the army, I went to complete my Bagrut tests and do a psychometric test, all in the name of my goal: to study education.

After I finished my Bagrut tests and before the psychometric test, I made an appointment with D, the pedagogical secretary of Shafririm high school to tell her, excitedly, that I wanted to be a teacher. I knew she was familiar with Seminar Hakibbutzim, and she knew a thing or two about academic teaching. I told myself she could strengthen me and help me.

At the meeting sat L, my guardian angel. I went to D and told her that I had chosen to become a teacher, that a teacher was what I wanted to be. L sat on the side, and I saw the excitement on his face. D said something to me that I wasn't prepared for, "You shouldn't bother, you won't succeed, you won't be able to take the pressure of academic studies, you should try something different. A temporary job will suit you more."

I was shocked into silence. How could it be that someone so senior would shatter the dream of a boy who wanted to be an educator? L got up. I'd never seen him angry until that moment. He told her, "You're talking nonsense! I know this boy, you don't, and if someone can be a teacher, it's him, and not you, you should be ashamed!" and took me outside.

At this stage, I had tears in my eyes. He said, "Look at me, you are going to go and study education, fulfill your dream, and you won't just be any teacher, you'll be the best teacher there is, all your students will love you, teachers will want to be like you, and you'll achieve anything you want because it's you and you can do it!"

If it wasn't for L who said those words to me, I do not believe I would have gone for it. But my guardian angel gave me my future again.

I did the psychometric, I scored too low, and I went to the exceptions committee. In the exceptions committee, I met Dr. DS and Gilat, the amazing lecturer writing this book. I was asked there what would happen if I was told I was not accepted to school here. I answered, "If I am not accepted here, I will search for another place that will accept me, not based on ten extra points in the psychometric test, but based on my desire and skills in education. Based on my way, and not on a number that does not represent or mean anything."

Even though you do not usually get given answers on the spot, Dr. DS, who was my pedagogical advisor in my first year in Seminar Hakibbutzim, ran after me and told me, "You've been accepted!"

My studies at Seminar Hakibbutzim were not simple, but I enjoyed every minute. I learned a lot. I met amazing lecturers who helped me and inspired me even more on my way to becoming a teacher. I met P, who was also my pedagogical guide for history and the one who made me fall in love with the subject that I teach for Bagrut tests until today. An amazing person!

I remember during my third year of studies, I was doing my practical work (teaching training) as a student of education in Shafririm school. D met me at the gate. The same D that did not believe in me then, and she gave me a hug. I did not hold a grudge, but in my heart, I said to myself, "I showed her."

I was lucky enough to become a student of a teacher-coach I knew, a teacher who held my hand through this whole path. I was a student of L, and I helped his class with history.

I met Doctor SF, today a professor, at the end of my B.ed., when doing a seminary class on Nietzsche in philosophy. SF, or as I called him, "my academic L," convinced me to do a master's degree without a thesis, something I had never even thought of since I had learning disabilities: how could I possibly do that?—But I did!

SF helped me in any way he could. He taught me that an educator can empower and contribute but also destroy (I remembered the homeroom teacher who ignored me in elementary school and how much I suffered). He taught me that an educator should not push the student toward success, but walk beside them, believe in them, and watch them succeed, like SF himself did.

Today I am a substitute homeroom teacher and a teacher of geography, writing skills, history (including for Bagrut tests), and civil studies (for Bagrut tests). I have B.ed. in special education with a specialty in history, and I have a master's in humanities.

I have been a teacher for six years, and I am now thinking about a thesis and doctorate. Who would have believed!

By the way, to my dear students that I love and adore with all my heart, I tell them in their first lesson with me, "Hello, it is nice to meet you, I am Itai, your teacher, and I have learning disabilities."

Today, I know I can do it because my teachers and lecturers helped me feel this way. I also pass this feeling on to my students. This is what it means to be a teacher and educator—to believe in your students and to help them succeed because they can.

This is the answer to the question of why I chose to be a teacher.

The issue here is not financial, the value is not financial, it is so much more.

I want to thank all the special people that made me who I am: my family, my amazing teachers L, S, LU, A, Y, B, YR, D. And my amazing lecturers, P, SP, Gilat, BS, S, N. You taught me what it means to be an educator, and that is what I am today.

To contact and request a lecture: itaybenyakar@gmail.com

FROM AGONY TO HARMONY

SHACHAR PERETZ MICHAEL

My name is Shachar Peretz Michael, and I am a student of special education and early childhood education. This is my story.

The girl in me is still alive and present. If I knew what she would go through and how she would cope, I would probably struggle to believe it. However, life is stranger than fiction, and it proved to me that everything is possible. Of course, as I am growing up and becoming a woman, and as I am writing this, I do not know what the future holds. I think that maybe this story isn't just about me, about Shachar as an individual. Maybe this is a story that can help a lot of people who are going or went through a mental crisis, and I have the opportunity to open a window for them into a new and better world. Your life story isn't what you have lived but how you tell it. This is true for the world, for nations, and for people. I decided to tell a story of a brave woman.

My name is Shachar.[22] It means the darkest moment before the morning light, and that has been my life. The day I emerged from darkness to light was the 9th of Av [Jewish fast day to mourn the destruction of the temple]. I was born on this day, a day of sadness and missing what could have been if there was no destruction. And, in fact, I also experienced internal destruction from which I was saved. I also experienced deep internal destruction from

---

22 Literally, the name means "dawn".

which I came out stronger and more connected to myself.

It was in 9th grade when my amazing psychiatrist approached my parents and delicately told them, "Your daughter has Bipolar Affective Disorder." My parents did not know what to do, but they understood that here was a challenge that needed to be dealt with.

A year later, I switched to learning in a special education program in a high school aimed at youths who have psychiatric disorders. In the beginning, I had trouble accepting the fact that I was joining a hidden circle of people struggling with mental health, but slowly I grew to accept it, and I got better, meaning I learned to deal with the challenges. I finished high school with twelve years of education but did not finish my Bagrut tests.

When I finished high school, I began my national service year. I was placed at a preschool,[23] and then I served in the army, in the Israeli navy. The military service was my start in life, the beginning of my independence. This move was a turning point for me. My faith in myself grew, as did the sense that someone would always be by my side. I felt empowered.

I finished the army with happiness, pride, honor, and belief in myself. However, along with happiness, fears came up. I very much wanted to advance in life. I wanted to learn, to develop, and, more than anything, to help people who were in the same situation I had been in special education. The goal was clear: to be an educator. But it was also clear that no learning institution would accept me as I was, since I had no Bagrut.

---

23 In this case, the text refers to ages 3 to 4.

I found a way in Eshnav Hamichlala Leminhal.[24] There I met the man who would become my husband and life partner. I also found an amazing option perfect for my situation: a special training college that would help me get to academic studies in special education and early childhood education. Today I am studying for my B.ed., and I am training to be a teacher in the field I dreamt of, in a college in Israel. My dreams and ambitions are bigger than ever, and the horizon is looking good.

I want to thank my parents, brothers, sisters, and everyone who believed in me in my hardest moment: your faith made me who I am today.

My message is: never give up! Even if you think things are lost, the sun will come up! Believe in yourself and always think how good things can be, contribute from your experience to the other and be happy with your life!

---

24 This is a program that helps potential students with learning disorders and other disabilities receive post high school education, find jobs, and get accepted into academic studies.

MY HEARTFELT THANKS

To my husband Itzik, and my children: Maya, Naama (RIP), and Yoav. For your endless faith in my ability to fulfill the dream, for the support, encouragement, and boundless love. You are my strength!

To my mother, Batia Sarig, and my father-in-law, Mordechai Trabelsi. For your faith in my ability and your pride in me. You are the wind beneath my wings!

To generations of students, teachers, coaches, and principals, who encouraged me to leave my mark and start writing as a gift to all those who seek to adapt insights from years of experience, with love and passion for education, teaching, shaping the future and the way. You are my inspiration, and you all have a place in my heart!

To the five stars that told their personal stories in the second part of the book, for everyone's benefit, with simplicity, modesty, and grace. You are my inner compass!

To the wonderful staff of Niv Books, your definition as a social publishing company fits the very vision of this book. You are my chance to give and to pass it forward!

To Micky Hib and the staff of the Colony Hotel in Haifa, who in this busy time gave me two weeks of peace and quiet to write, with warmth and caring for my needs. Thank you for your open hearts and giving!

To you, readers,

If you have come this far, you have really read everything.

I hope you have been inspired, empowered, and encouraged for the things you are already doing, and that you have gotten a boost to do more, much more, of all this good. Thank you for your trust!

I'd be happy to read your comments, requests, and suggestions about topics you would like me to write more about in the future.

Find me on Amazon as Gilat Trabelsi
Yours, Gilat

Printed in Great Britain
by Amazon